T0024216

ESCAPE THE RAT RACE

Learn How Money Works and Become a Rich Kid

Robert Kiyosaki

Author of bestseller *Rich Dad Poor Dad*

If you purchase this book without a cover, or purchase a PDF, jpg, or tiff copy of this book, it is likely stolen property or a counterfeit. In that case, neither the authors, the publisher, nor any of their employees or agents has received any payment for the copy. Furthermore, counterfeiting is a known avenue of financial support for organized crime and terrorist groups. We urge you to please not purchase any such copy and to report any instance of someone selling such copies to Plata Publishing LLC.

This publication is designed to provide competent and reliable information regarding the subject matter covered. However, it is sold with the understanding that the author and publisher are not engaged in rendering legal, financial, or other professional advice. Laws and practices often vary from state to state and country to country and if legal or other expert assistance is required, the services of a professional should be sought. The author and publisher specifically disclaim any liability that is incurred from the use or application of the contents of this book.

Some material in this book is adapted from *Rich Dad Poor Dad*. Although based on a true story, certain events in this book have been fictionalized for educational content and impact.

Copyright © 2005, 2012 by Robert T. Kiyosaki. All rights reserved. Except as permitted under the U.S. Copyright Act of 1976, no part of this publication may be reproduced, distributed, or transmitted in any form or by any means or stored in a database or retrieval system, without the prior written permission of the publisher.

Published by Plata Publishing, LLC

CASHFLOW, Rich Dad, and Rich Kid Smart Kid are registered trademarks of CASHFLOW Technologies, Inc.

is a registered trademark of CASHFLOW Technologies, Inc.

Plata Publishing, LLC
4330 N. Civic Center Plaza
Suite 100
Scottsdale, AZ 85251
(480) 998-6971

Visit our websites: PlataPublishing.com and RichDad.com

Printed in the United States of America
First Edition: January 2005
First Plata Publishing Edition: November 2012
ISBN: 978-1-61268-055-2

CREATIVE CREDITS: Rantz Hoseley | Writer & Inks
Ben Plouffe | Penciler, Colorist
Michael Yamada | Penciler
Cory Nelson | Writer
James Offredi | Colorist
Blambot's NatePiekos | Letterer

Best-Selling Books and Games by Robert T. Kiyosaki

BOOKS

Rich Dad Poor Dad
What the Rich Teach Their Kids About Money –
That the Poor and Middle Class Do Not

Rich Dad's CASHFLOW Quadrant
Guide to Financial Freedom

Rich Dad's Guide to Investing
What the Rich Invest In That the Poor and Middle Class Do Not

Rich Dad's Rich Kid Smart Kid
Give Your Child a Financial Head Start

Rich Dad's Retire Young Retire Rich
How to Get Rich and Stay Rich

Rich Dad's Prophecy
Why the Biggest Stock Market Crash in History Is Still Coming...
And How You Can Prepare Yourself and Profit from It!

Rich Dad's Success Stories
Real-Life Success Stories from Real-Life People
Who Followed the Rich Dad Lessons

Rich Dad's Guide to Becoming Rich
Without Cutting Up Your Credit Cards
Turn Bad Debt into Good Debt

Rich Dad's Who Took My Money?
Why Slow Investors Lose and Fast Money Wins!

Rich Dad Poor Dad for Teens
The Secrets About Money – That You Don't Learn in School!

Rich Dad's Escape the Rat Race
Learn How Money Works and Become a Rich Kid

Rich Dad's Before You Quit Your Job
Ten Real-Life Lessons Every Entrepreneur Should Know
About Building a Multimillion-Dollar Business

Rich Dad's Increase Your Financial IQ
Get Smarter with Your Money

Conspiracy of the Rich
The 8 New Rules of Money

Unfair Advantage
The Power of Financial Education

GAMES

CASHFLOW® for Kids

CASHFLOW® 101

CASHFLOW® 202

1

Meet Tina, Tim and Red

ESCAPE THE RAT RACE
HOT DOGS
TICKETS
BUMPER CARS
Tim
Red
Tina
HEY DUDE, LET'S GO OVER TO THE ELIMINATOR!
OH MAN, IT'S S'POSED TO BE SO FAST, IT'LL MAKE YOUR EYEBALLS POP OUT!
LET'S DO IT!

TICKETS
OH MAN, YOU ARE SO GOING DOWN!
NOT EVEN!
ALL RIGHT GUYS, FIVE BUCKS.
TICKETS
HERE YA GO, MAN.
OH MAN, THIS IS GONNA BE GREAT!
I'D LIKE...
UMMMM...
NEXT!

GO AHEAD WITHOUT ME, GUYS. I'LL WAIT HERE.
UGH, THIS STINKS! I'M ALWAYS RUNNING OUT OF MONEY.
RED ALWAYS SEEMS TO HAVE MONEY, AND HE'S GOT A JOB...
HOT DOGS
HELP WANTED
THAT'S IT-I'LL GET A JOB!
IF I HAVE A JOB, I'LL BE MAKING TRUCKLOADS OF MONEY! ALL THE GUYS WILL BE SO JEALOUS, 'CAUSE I'LL BE THE GUY WITH THE BIG BUCKS AND ALL OF THE REALLY COOL STUFF...

WOW, THAT WAS GREAT!
MY TEETH ARE STILL RATTLING!
HEY RED, I THINK I'M GOING TO CATCH UP WITH YOU GUYS LATER.
WELL, I'M HEADING OVER TO THE "RIPPER." YOU COMING RED?
GO AHEAD, I'LL MEET YOU OVER THERE IN A MINUTE.
WHY AREN'T YOU COMING WITH US, MAN? WHAT'S UP?
I CAN'T GO ON ANY MORE RIDES, SINCE I'M OUT OF CASH.
HOT DOGS
HELP WANTED!
SO, I FIGURED SINCE YOUR JOB GIVES YOU ENOUGH MONEY TO GO ON ALL THE RIDES, I THOUGHT MAYBE I'D GET A JOB, TOO. THAT WAY I WON'T HAVE TO WORRY ABOUT MONEY ANYMORE. I'LL BE RICH!
BWAHA HAHAHA!

WHA...WHAT'S SO FUNNY?
WAIT-YOU HONESTLY THINK THAT YOU'RE GONNA GET A JOB AND THEN SUDDENLY BECOME RICH?
WELL... YEAH. I MEAN, YOU'VE GOT A JOB AND YOU'RE ABLE TO GO ON ALL THE RIDES.
YEAH, BUT IT'S NOT MY JOB ALONE THAT MAKES ME MY MONEY.
IT ISN'T?
LOOK, DON'T YOU REMEMBER LAST YEAR WHEN I TOOK THAT SUMMER JOB?
OH YEAH, I DO. YOU WERE TRYING TO BUY THAT BIKE. MAN, YOU WERE EVEN WORKING WEEKENDS.
EXACTLY. I FIGURED IF I GOT THAT SUMMER JOB I'D BE RICH IN NO TIME.
THE PROBLEM WAS, I WORKED ALL SUMMER LONG, BUT NO MATTER HOW HARD I WORKED, I NEVER SEEMED TO HAVE ENOUGH MONEY TO BUY IT--MUCH LESS GET RICH.

BUT, YOU HAVE MONEY NOW... SO, I GUESS YOUR NEW JOB PAYS YOU MORE.
NOPE! SEE, AFTER A SUMMER OF WORKING REALLY HARD, I REALIZED THAT WHAT I WAS DOING OBVIOUSLY WASN'T WORKING.
I REALIZED THERE WERE A LOT OF HARD-WORKING PEOPLE OUT THERE. THEY WORK LONG HOURS, WEEKENDS AND A LOT OF THEM GET PAY RAISES.
PAYROLL
BUT, AT THE END OF THE DAY, MOST OF THEM STILL COMPLAINED ABOUT NOT HAVING ENOUGH MONEY.
SO, IF WORKING REALLY HARD AT A GOOD JOB ISN'T MAKING ALL OF THEM RICH, WHAT MADE ME THINK IT WAS GONNA MAKE ME RICH?
BUT RED, I GOTTA SAY, I DON'T GET IT...IF YOU DON'T GET RICH FROM A JOB, HOW DO YOU GET RICH?

WELL, RATHER THAN JUST ACCEPT THAT I WAS NEVER GOING TO BE RICH, I DECIDED THAT I NEEDED TO LEARN ABOUT MONEY. I NEEDED TO HAVE ***FINANCIAL INTELLIGENCE.***
FINANCIAL INTELLIGENCE?
FINANCIAL INTELLIGENCE IS WHAT SEPARATES THE PEOPLE WHO HAVE MONEY AND KEEP GETTING MORE FROM PEOPLE WHO WISH THEY HAD MONEY AND NEVER SEEM TO HAVE ENOUGH.
UNEMPLOYMENT
TAXES
BILLS
DEBT
INTEREST RATES
FINANCIAL INTELLIGENCE HELPS YOU SEE HOW MONEY WORKS, AND HOW TO MAKE IT WORK FOR YOU-RATHER THAN YOU WORKING FOR IT.
IT'S THE KIND OF INTELLIGENCE THAT SHOWS YOU HOW TO MAKE SURE YOU'RE NEVER WITHOUT MONEY-- AND HOW TO KEEP MONEY FLOWING INTO YOUR POCKETS. ALL WITHOUT YOU HAVING TO WORK AT A JOB IN ORDER TO GET IT.

WOW, THAT SOUNDS REALLY COMPLICATED.
BUT MY GRADES ARE HORRIBLE, AND I'VE NEVER BEEN VERY GOOD IN SCHOOL. NOW I KNOW FOR A FACT THAT I'LL NEVER GET RICH!
I KNOW IT MAY SEEM LIKE THAT AT FIRST, BUT THERE ARE ONLY A FEW BASIC LESSONS YOU NEED TO LEARN. ANYONE CAN DO IT.
THIS IS FINANCIAL EDUCATION. DON'T THINK OF IT AS THE SAME STUFF YOU LEARN IN SCHOOL. THEY DON'T TEACH THIS IN SCHOOL. ANYONE CAN LEARN IT.
UM, WAIT A SEC... YOU MEAN, I DON'T HAVE TO BE REALLY SMART TO GET RICH?
NOPE.
SWEET! NO MORE SCHOOL FOR ME!
WHOA, WHOA DUDE... SLOW DOWN THERE MAN... YOU STILL NEED SCHOOL. IT GIVES YOU OTHER TYPES OF INFORMATION AND SKILLS YOU'LL NEED. IT'S JUST NOT EVERYTHING YOU NEED.
OH. WELL, A GUY CAN HOPE CAN'T HE? SO, HOW EXACTLY DO I BECOME RICH?

2

Robert's Story

Red

LET ME TELL YOU ABOUT A BOOK I READ CALLED ***RICH DAD POOR DAD*** BY ROBERT KIYOSAKI. ALTHOUGH ROBERT IS RICH AND FAMOUS NOW, IN 1956, HE WAS JUST ANOTHER KID, TRYING TO FIGURE OUT HOW TO MAKE MONEY TO BUY THE THINGS HE WANTED, LIKE COMIC BOOKS AND ICE CREAM.

DAD, CAN YOU TELL ME HOW TO GET RICH?

ROBERT'S DAD WAS A TEACHER. BUT EVEN THOUGH HE WAS REALLY SMART AND HAD A GOOD JOB, HE DIDN'T HAVE MUCH MONEY.
WELL, SON, IF YOU WANT TO BE RICH, YOU HAVE TO LEARN TO MAKE MONEY.
BUT... HOW DO I MAKE MONEY?
WELL, USE YOUR HEAD, SON.
WHICH REALLY MEANT, "THAT'S ALL I'M GOING TO TELL YOU," OR "I DON'T KNOW THE ANSWER, SO DON'T EMBARRASS ME."
THE NEXT MORNING, ROBERT TOLD HIS BEST FRIEND, MIKE, WHAT HIS DAD HAD SAID. THEY CAME UP WITH A PLAN.
SO THAT SATURDAY MORNING, MIKE BECAME HIS FIRST BUSINESS PARTNER.
MIKE HAD GOTTEN AN INSPIRATION FROM A BOOK HE HAD READ, SO THEY STARTED A BUSINESS. FOR THE NEXT SEVERAL WEEKS, MIKE AND ROBERT RAN AROUND THEIR NEIGHBORHOOD, KNOCKING ON DOORS...
... ASKING THEIR NEIGHBORS IF THEY COULD HAVE THEIR USED TOOTHPASTE TUBES.
SOME ASKED WHAT THEY WERE DOING, BUT ROBERT AND MIKE JUST SAID, "WE CAN'T TELL YOU. IT'S A BUSINESS SECRET."

WHEN THEY HAD ENOUGH TUBES, THEY STARTED PRODUCTION.
THE ASSEMBLY LINE WAS CREATED IN ROBERT'S DRIVEWAY.
ROBERT'S DAD AND A FRIEND OF HIS SHOWED UP TO FIND THE PRODUCTION IN FULL SWING.
SEE, BACK IN 1956 TOOTHPASTE DIDN'T COME IN PLASTIC TUBES...
IT CAME IN LEAD TUBES. MELTING THE LEAD TUBES WAS THE KEY TO ROBERT AND MIKE'S IDEA OF HOW TO MAKE THEM RICH.

CAREFUL....

WHAT'S IN THOSE PLASTER MOLDS?
WATCH...

THIS SHOULD BE A GOOD BATCH.

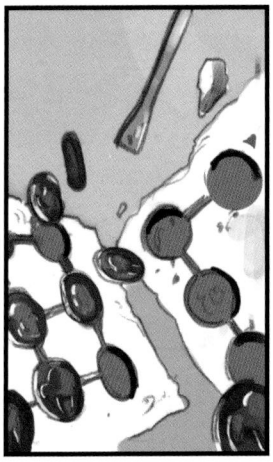

OH NO! YOU'RE CASTING NICKELS OUT OF LEAD!
THAT'S RIGHT!
WE'RE DOING WHAT YOU TOLD US... WE'RE MAKING MONEY!

THE FRIEND OF ROBERT'S DAD COULDN'T HELP BUT TO LAUGH AT WHAT THE BOYS HAD DONE.
LET THEM GO! THEY MIGHT BE DEVELOPING A NATURAL TALENT!

...BUT ROBERT'S FATHER SAT THE BOYS DOWN AND TOLD THEM THE MEANING OF THE WORD COUNTERFEITING.

I GUESS JIMMY AND HIS FRIENDS ARE RIGHT. WE ARE POOR.

BOYS, YOU'RE ONLY POOR IF YOU GIVE UP. THE MOST IMPORTANT THING IS THAT YOU DID SOMETHING. MOST PEOPLE ONLY TALK AND DREAM OF GETTING RICH. YOU'VE DONE SOMETHING.
I'M VERY PROUD OF THE TWO OF YOU. KEEP GOING. DON'T QUIT.

SO HOW COME YOU'RE NOT RICH, DAD?

BECAUSE I CHOSE TO BE A SCHOOLTEACHER. SCHOOL-TEACHERS REALLY DON'T THINK ABOUT BEING RICH. WE JUST LIKE TO TEACH. IF YOU BOYS WANT TO LEARN HOW TO BE RICH, TALK TO YOUR DAD, MIKE.

MY DAD?

YEAH, YOUR DAD AND I HAVE THE SAME BANKER, AND HE RAVES ABOUT YOUR FATHER.
HE TELLS ME THAT YOUR FATHER IS BRILLIANT WHEN IT COMES TO MAKING MONEY.

THEN HOW COME WE DON'T HAVE A NICE CAR AND A NICE HOUSE LIKE THE RICH KIDS AT SCHOOL?

HAVING A NICE CAR AND A NICE HOUSE DOESN'T MEAN YOU'RE RICH OR THAT YOU KNOW HOW TO MAKE MONEY.

JIMMY'S DAD WORKS FOR THE SUGAR PLANTATION. HE'S NOT MUCH DIFFERENT FROM ME. HE WORKS FOR A COMPANY, AND I WORK FOR THE GOVERNMENT. THE COMPANY BUYS THE CAR FOR HIM. BUT THE SUGAR COMPANY IS IN FINANCIAL TROUBLE, AND JIMMY'S DAD MAY SOON HAVE NOTHING.
YOUR DAD IS DIFFERENT, MIKE. HE SEEMS TO BE BUILDING AN EMPIRE, AND I SUSPECT IN A FEW YEARS HE WILL BE A VERY RICH MAN.

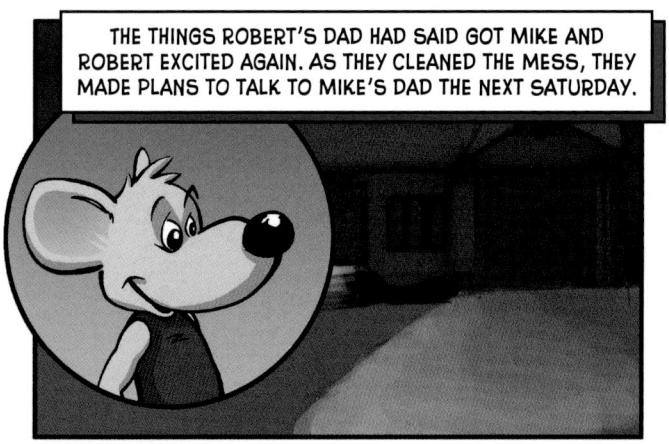
THE THINGS ROBERT'S DAD HAD SAID GOT MIKE AND ROBERT EXCITED AGAIN. AS THEY CLEANED THE MESS, THEY MADE PLANS TO TALK TO MIKE'S DAD THE NEXT SATURDAY.

SO, AT 7:30 ON SATURDAY MORNING, ROBERT CAUGHT THE BUS TO THE POOR SIDE OF TOWN.

C'MON, FOLLOW ME.

WHO ARE THOSE PEOPLE?
OH, THEY WORK FOR MY DAD.

THE OLDER MAN RUNS HIS WAREHOUSES, AND THE WOMEN ARE THE MANAGERS OF THE RESTAURANTS. AND YOU SAW THE CONSTRUCTION SUPERVISOR WHO'S WORKING ON A ROAD PROJECT ABOUT FIFTY MILES FROM HERE.
DOES THIS GO ON ALL THE TIME?
NOT ALWAYS, BUT A LOT.

SO, WHAT EXACTLY DID YOU SAY TO YOUR DAD?
I ASKED HIM IF HE WOULD TEACH US HOW TO MAKE MONEY.

WHAT DID HE SAY TO THAT?
WELL, HE GRINNED AND SAID HE WOULD MAKE US AN OFFER.

READY, BOYS?

MIKE SAYS YOU WANT TO LEARN TO MAKE MONEY. IS THAT CORRECT, ROBERT?

YES, SIR.

OK, HERE'S MY OFFER. I'LL TEACH YOU, BUT I WON'T DO IT CLASS-ROOM-STYLE. YOU WORK FOR ME, I'LL TEACH YOU. YOU DON'T WORK FOR ME, I WON'T TEACH YOU.

I CAN TEACH YOU FASTER IF YOU WORK, AND I'M WASTING MY TIME IF YOU JUST WANT TO SIT AND LISTEN LIKE YOU DO IN SCHOOL. THAT'S MY OFFER. TAKE IT OR LEAVE IT.
TAKE IT.
TAKE IT.

GOOD. MRS. MARTIN WILL BE BY IN TEN MINUTES. AFTER I'M THROUGH WITH HER, YOU CAN RIDE WITH HER TO MY SUPERETTE AND START WORKING.
I'LL PAY YOU 10 CENTS AN HOUR AND YOU'LL WORK FOR THREE HOURS EVERY SATURDAY.

BUT I HAVE A SOFTBALL GAME TODAY.

TAKE IT...
...OR LEAVE IT.

I'LL TAKE IT.

PASSING UP SOFTBALL WAS TOUGH FOR ROBERT.
BUT HE KNEW THAT IF IT MEANT HE COULD BE RICH SOMEDAY, IT'D BE WORTH IT.

THE NEXT SATURDAY MORNING, MIKE AND ROBERT WERE WORKING FOR MRS. MARTIN.
SHE WAS A NICE WOMAN AND SAID THAT MIKE AND ROBERT REMINDED HER OF HER TWO SONS WHO HAD GROWN UP.
ICE CREAM
SHE WAS A TASK MASTER, THOUGH. THEY SPENT THREE HOURS TAKING CANS OFF THE SHELVES AND BRUSHING EACH CAN TO GET THE DUST OFF. THEN THEY HAD TO RE-STACK THEM NEATLY.
IT WAS EXCRUCIATING, BORING WORK.
MIKE'S DAD OWNED NINE OF THESE LITTLE SUPERETTES. THEY WERE LITTLE NEIGHBORHOOD GROCERY STORES WHERE PEOPLE BOUGHT STUFF LIKE MILK AND BREAD.
THE PROBLEM WAS, THIS WAS HAWAII--AND IN THE DAYS BEFORE AIR CONDITIONING, STORES COULD NOT CLOSE THEIR DOORS BECAUSE OF THE HEAT.
EVERY TIME A CAR DROVE BY, DUST WOULD SWIRL AND SETTLE IN THE STORE.
SO THEY HAD A JOB AS LONG AS THERE WAS NO AIR CONDITIONING.

FOR THREE WEEKS, MIKE AND ROBERT WORKED FOR THREE HOURS EACH SATURDAY. BY NOON, WORK WAS OVER, AND MRS. MARTIN DROPPED THREE DIMES IN EACH OF THEIR HANDS.
NOW, EVEN AT THE AGE OF NINE IN THE MID-1950S, 30 CENTS WASN'T TOO EXCITING. COMIC BOOKS COST 10 CENTS BACK THEN, SO ROBERT USUALLY SPENT HIS MONEY ON COMIC BOOKS AND WENT HOME.
FOUR WEEKS LATER, ROBERT WAS READY TO QUIT. HE HAD AGREED TO WORK ONLY BECAUSE HE WANTED TO LEARN TO MAKE MONEY FROM MIKE'S DAD, AND NOW HE FELT LIKE A SLAVE.
ON TOP OF THAT, HE HADN'T SEEN MIKE'S DAD SINCE THAT FIRST SATURDAY.
I'M QUITTING! SCHOOL IS BORING AND NOW I DON'T EVEN HAVE SATURDAYS TO LOOK FORWARD TO.
AND ALL FOR 30 LOUSY CENTS!
WHAT? WHAT IS IT?
DAD SAID THIS WOULD HAPPEN. HE SAID TO MEET WITH HIM WHEN YOU WERE READY TO QUIT.
WHAT?! HE'S BEEN WAITING FOR ME TO GET FED UP?
SORT OF. DAD'S KIND OF DIFFERENT. HE TEACHES DIFFERENTLY FROM YOUR DAD. YOUR MOM AND DAD LECTURE A LOT.
JUST WAIT TILL THIS SATURDAY. I'LL TELL HIM YOU'RE READY.
YOU MEAN I'VE BEEN SET UP?
NO, NOT REALLY, BUT... MAYBE. ANYWAY, DAD WILL EXPLAIN ON SATURDAY.

3

Robert Escapes the Trap

Tim

SO, AT EIGHT O'CLOCK THAT SATURDAY MORNING, ROBERT FOUND HIMSELF AT MIKE'S HOUSE AGAIN.
TAKE A SEAT AND WAIT IN LINE.
ROBERT FELT AWKWARD WAITING TO TALK TO MIKE'S DAD, BUT HE WAS DETERMINED TO GET WHAT HE DESERVED, SO HE SAT DOWN AND WAITED.
WAITED 20 MINUTES AS THE OLDER MAN SITTING NEXT TO HIM WENT IN TO TALK TO MIKE'S DAD...
WAITED 40 MINUTES AS THE NICE LADY WHO HAD OFFERED HIM A SEAT WENT IN TO TALK TO MIKE'S DAD...
WAITED UNTIL HE WAS STEAMING MAD-- AND THE ONLY PERSON STILL WAITING.
ROBERT COULD HEAR MIKE'S DAD TALKING ON THE PHONE, RUSTLING PAPERS...
...IGNORING HIM.

FINALLY, AT EXACTLY NINE O'CLOCK, MIKE'S DAD CAME OUT, SAID NOTHING, AND SIGNALED FOR ROBERT TO ENTER HIS OFFICE.

I UNDERSTAND YOU WANT A RAISE, OR YOU'RE GOING TO QUIT.

WELL, YOU'RE NOT KEEPING YOUR END OF THE BARGAIN! YOU SAID THAT YOU WOULD TEACH ME IF I WORKED FOR YOU. WELL, I'VE WORKED FOR YOU.

I'VE WORKED HARD. I'VE GIVEN UP MY SOFTBALL GAMES TO WORK FOR YOU AND YOU DON'T KEEP YOUR WORD.
YOU HAVEN'T TAUGHT ME ***ANYTHING.*** YOU'RE A ***CROOK*** LIKE EVERYONE IN TOWN THINKS YOU ARE.

YOU'RE GREEDY. YOU WANT ALL THE MONEY AND DON'T TAKE CARE OF YOUR EMPLOYEES. YOU MAKE ME WAIT AND DON'T SHOW ME ANY RESPECT.
I'M ONLY A LITTLE BOY, AND I DESERVE TO BE TREATED BETTER.

NOT BAD... IN LESS THAN A MONTH, YOU SOUND LIKE MOST OF MY EMPLOYEES.

WHAT?! I THOUGHT YOU WERE GOING TO KEEP YOUR END OF THE BARGAIN AND TEACH ME.

I ***AM*** TEACHING YOU.

WHAT HAVE YOU TAUGHT ME? NOTHING! YOU HAVEN'T EVEN TALKED TO ME ONCE SINCE I AGREED TO WORK FOR PEANUTS. TEN CENTS AN HOUR! HAH!

I SHOULD NOTIFY THE GOVERNMENT ABOUT YOU! WE HAVE CHILD LABOR LAWS, YOU KNOW. MY DAD WORKS FOR THE GOVERNMENT!

NOW YOU SOUND JUST LIKE MOST OF THE PEOPLE WHO USED TO WORK FOR ME. PEOPLE I'VE EITHER FIRED... OR THEY'VE QUIT.
HOW DO YOU KNOW THAT I'VE NOT TAUGHT YOU ANYTHING?

WELL, YOU'VE NEVER TALKED TO ME. I'VE WORKED FOR THREE WEEKS, AND YOU HAVEN'T TAUGHT ME A THING!

DOES TEACHING MEAN TALKING OR LECTURING TO YOU?

THAT'S HOW THEY TEACH YOU IN SCHOOL, BUT THAT'S NOT HOW LIFE TEACHES YOU, AND I WOULD SAY THAT LIFE IS THE BEST TEACHER OF ALL.

YOU BOYS ARE THE FIRST PEOPLE WHO HAVE EVER ASKED ME TO TEACH THEM HOW TO MAKE MONEY. I HAVE MORE THAN 150 EMPLOYEES, AND NOT ONE OF THEM HAS ASKED ME WHAT I KNOW ABOUT MONEY.
SO MOST WILL SPEND THE BEST YEARS OF THEIR LIVES WORKING FOR MONEY, BUT NOT REALLY UNDERSTANDING WHAT IT IS THEY'RE WORKING FOR.

SO WHEN MIKE TOLD ME ABOUT YOU WANTING TO LEARN TO MAKE MONEY, I DECIDED TO DESIGN A COURSE THAT WAS CLOSE TO REAL LIFE. THAT'S WHY I ONLY PAID YOU 10 CENTS.

SO WHAT'S THE LESSON I LEARNED FROM WORKING FOR ONLY 10 CENTS AN HOUR? THAT YOU'RE CHEAP, AND TAKE ADVANTAGE OF YOUR WORKERS?

SEE, YOU THINK *I'M* THE PROBLEM. THAT'S WHAT MOST PEOPLE DO WHEN THEY FIND THEY CAN'T PAY THEIR BILLS.
THEY BLAME THEIR BOSS FOR NOT PAYING THEM ENOUGH AND GO LOOKING FOR A BETTER JOB.

SO WHAT AM I SUPPOSED TO DO, JUST TAKE THIS MEASLY 10 CENTS AN HOUR AND SMILE?

THAT'S WHAT THE OTHER PEOPLE DO. JUST ACCEPT A PAYCHECK AND WAIT FOR A RAISE, THINKING THAT MORE MONEY WILL SOLVE THE PROBLEM.
JUST LOOK AT YOUR DAD. HE MAKES A LOT OF MONEY, AND HE STILL CAN'T PAY HIS BILLS.
SO WHAT DO I *DO*, THEN?

YOU NEED TO START USING *THIS*--THE STUFF BETWEEN YOUR EARS.

I HAVE KEPT MY PROMISE. I'VE BEEN TEACHING YOU FROM AFAR. AT NINE YEARS OLD, YOU'VE GOTTEN A TASTE OF WHAT IT FEELS LIKE TO WORK FOR MONEY. JUST MULTIPLY YOUR LAST MONTH BY FIFTY YEARS AND YOU'LL HAVE AN IDEA OF WHAT MOST PEOPLE SPEND THEIR LIVES DOING.

HOW DID YOU FEEL WAITING IN LINE TO SEE ME?
TERRIBLE.
AND HOW DID YOU FEEL WHEN MRS. MARTIN DROPPED THREE DIMES IN YOUR HAND FOR THREE HOURS WORK?
I FELT LIKE IT WASN'T ENOUGH. IT SEEMED LIKE NOTHING. I WAS DISAPPOINTED.
THAT'S HOW MOST EMPLOYEES FEEL WHEN THEY LOOK AT THEIR PAYCHECKS. ESPECIALLY AFTER ALL THE TAX AND OTHER DEDUCTIONS ARE TAKEN OUT. AT LEAST YOU GOT 100%.

YOU MEAN MOST WORKERS DON'T GET PAID EVERYTHING?

HEAVENS, NO! THE GOVERNMENT TAKES ITS SHARE FIRST. YOU'RE TAXED WHEN YOU EARN. YOU'RE TAXED WHEN YOU SPEND. YOU'RE TAXED WHEN YOU SAVE. YOU'RE TAXED WHEN YOU DIE.

AS I SAID, THERE'S A LOT TO LEARN. LEARNING HOW TO HAVE MONEY WORK FOR YOU IS A LIFETIME STUDY.

SO, DO YOU STILL HAVE THE PASSION TO LEARN?
YOU BET!
GOOD. NOW GET BACK TO WORK. THIS TIME, I WILL PAY YOU NOTHING.
WHAT?!

YOU HEARD ME. NOTHING. YOU'LL WORK THE SAME THREE HOURS EVERY SATURDAY, BUT THIS TIME YOU WON'T BE PAID 10 CENTS PER HOUR.
YOU SAID YOU WANTED TO LEARN NOT TO WORK FOR MONEY, SO I'M NOT GOING TO PAY YOU ANYTHING.
THAT'S NOT FAIR! YOU'VE GOT TO PAY SOMETHING.
I'VE ALREADY HAD THIS CONVERSATION WITH MIKE. HE'S ALREADY WORKING, DUSTING AND STACKING CANNED GOODS FOR FREE.

YOU SAID YOU WANTED TO LEARN. IF YOU DON'T LEARN THIS NOW, YOU'LL GROW UP TO BE LIKE THE PEOPLE SITTING IN MY LIVING ROOM, WORKING FOR MONEY AND HOPING I DON'T FIRE THEM. HOPING MORE MONEY WILL SOLVE THE PROBLEM...
...OR YOU CAN DO WHAT MOST PEOPLE GROW UP TO DO - COMPLAIN THAT THERE IS NOT ENOUGH PAY, QUIT, AND GO LOOKING FOR ANOTHER JOB.
BUT WHAT DO I DO?
USE YOUR HEAD. IF YOU USE IT WELL, YOU'LL SOON THANK ME FOR GIVING YOU AN OPPORTUNITY, AND YOU'LL GROW INTO A RICH MAN.
NOW, GET OUT OF HERE AND GET BACK TO WORK.

FOR THREE MORE WEEKS, MIKE AND ROBERT WORKED FOR THREE HOURS, EVERY SATURDAY, FOR NOTHING. ROBERT DIDN'T TELL HIS DAD HE WASN'T BEING PAID. HE WOULDN'T HAVE UNDERSTOOD.
OVER TIME, THE WORK ROUTINE GOT EASIER. BUT THEY WERE STILL SAD TO BE MISSING SOFTBALL GAMES AND NOT BEING ABLE TO AFFORD A FEW COMIC BOOKS.
THREE WEEKS LATER, MIKE'S DAD MET THEM AT THE STORE.
HOW'S IT GOING, BOYS?
OK...
YEAH, OK.
LEARN ANYTHING YET?
WELL, YOU BOYS HAD BETTER START THINKING. YOU'RE STARING AT ONE OF LIFE'S BIGGEST LESSONS.
LET'S GO FOR A WALK.
IF YOU LEARN THE LESSON, YOU'LL ENJOY A LIFE OF GREAT FREEDOM AND SECURITY. IF YOU DON'T LEARN THE LESSON, YOU'LL WIND UP LIKE MRS. MARTIN AND MOST OF THE PEOPLE PLAYING SOFTBALL IN THIS PARK.
THEY WORK VERY HARD, FOR LITTLE MONEY, CLINGING TO THE ILLUSION OF JOB SECURITY, LOOKING FORWARD TO A TWO TO THREE-WEEK VACATION EACH YEAR AND A SKIMPY PENSION AFTER FORTY-FIVE YEARS OF WORK.
IF THAT EXCITES YOU, I'LL GIVE YOU A RAISE TO 25 CENTS AN HOUR.

DOESN'T THAT 25 CENTS AN HOUR SOUND GOOD? DOESN'T IT MAKE YOUR HEART BEAT A LITTLE FASTER?
NO.
BUT IT WAS TEMPTING TO ROBERT. AT THE TIME, 25 CENTS WAS BIG BUCKS.
OK, HOW ABOUT IF I PAY YOU A DOLLAR, THEN.
NO.
BUT ROBERT'S BRAIN WAS SCREAMING; "TAKE IT, TAKE IT!"
OK, $2 AN HOUR.
IN 1956, GETTING PAID $2 AN HOUR WOULD HAVE MADE ROBERT THE RICHEST KID IN THE WORLD.
HE COULD SEE IN HIS MIND ALL THE THINGS THAT KIND OF MONEY COULD GET HIM. A NEW BIKE, A NEW BASEBALL GLOVE, STACKS OF COMICS.
BUT SOMEHOW HE MANAGED TO KEEP HIS MOUTH SHUT.
OK, $5 AN HOUR.

NOW, IN 1956, NOT TOO MANY ADULTS MADE $5 AN HOUR. HE KNEW THAT IF MIKE'S DAD WAS OFFERING THAT MUCH, WHATEVER HE WAS GOING TO TEACH HIM HAD TO BE WORTH IT.
NO.
A FEELING OF CALM CAME OVER THEM, AND SUDDENLY THE TEMPTATION DISAPPEARED.
GOOD.
MOST PEOPLE HAVE A PRICE.
ONCE THEY GET THAT FIRST PAYCHECK, THEY START THINKING ABOUT ALL THE WONDERFUL THINGS THEY CAN BUY WITH THE MONEY.
BEFORE LONG, THEY'VE SPENT A LIFETIME WORKING, BUT NOT REALLY UNDERSTANDING WHAT THEY'RE WORKING FOR.
I WANT YOU TO AVOID THAT TRAP. THAT'S REALLY WHAT I WANT TO TEACH YOU.
I WANT TO TEACH YOU HOW TO AVOID THE RAT RACE. NOT JUST TO BE RICH, BECAUSE BEING RICH DOESN'T SOLVE THE PROBLEM.
IT DOESN'T?
NO, IT DOESN'T.

IT'S LIKE A DONKEY, DRAGGING A CART, WITH ITS OWNER DANGLING A CARROT JUST IN FRONT OF ITS NOSE.

THE DONKEY'S OWNER MAY BE GOING WHERE HE WANTS TO GO, BUT THE DONKEY IS CHASING AN ILLUSION. TOMORROW THERE WILL ONLY BE ANOTHER CARROT FOR THE DONKEY.

YOU MEAN THE MOMENT I BEGAN TO PICTURE A NEW BASEBALL GLOVE, CANDY, AND TOYS, THAT'S LIKE A CARROT TO A DONKEY?

EXACTLY. AND AS YOU GET OLDER, YOUR TOYS GET MORE EXPENSIVE. A NEW CAR, A BOAT, AND A BIG HOUSE TO IMPRESS YOUR FRIENDS. THAT'S THE TRAP.

SO, WHAT'S THE ANSWER?

YOU NEED TO OPEN YOUR MIND AND START LOOKING FOR OPPORTUNITIES.
TO LIVE A LIFE DICTATED BY THE SIZE OF A PAYCHECK IS NOT REALLY A LIFE. THINKING THAT A JOB WILL MAKE YOU FEEL SECURE IS LYING TO YOURSELF.

KEEP USING YOUR BRAIN, AND SOON YOU'LL SEE THINGS THAT OTHER PEOPLE NEVER SEE. OPPORTUNITIES RIGHT IN FRONT OF THEIR NOSES.
THE MOMENT YOU SEE ONE OPPORTUNITY, YOU'LL SEE THEM FOR THE REST OF YOUR LIFE.

FOR TWO MORE WEEKS ROBERT AND MIKE KEPT THINKING, TALKING, AND WORKING FOR FREE.
AT THE END OF THE SECOND SATURDAY, ROBERT SAW MRS. MARTIN CUTTING THE FRONT PAGE OF THE COMIC BOOKS IN HALF. ROBERT ASKED HER WHAT SHE WAS DOING.
I GIVE THE TOP HALF OF THE COVER BACK TO THE COMIC-BOOK DISTRIBUTOR FOR CREDIT WHEN HE BRINGS IN THE NEW COMICS AND I THROW THE REST OF THE BOOK AWAY.
HE'S COMING IN AN HOUR.
WHEN THE DISTRIBUTOR ARRIVED, ROBERT ASKED HIM IF THEY COULD KEEP THE COMIC BOOKS.
YOU CAN HAVE THEM IF YOU KEEP WORKING FOR THIS STORE AND DON'T SELL THEM.
AFTER CLEANING OUT THE BASEMENT AT MIKE'S HOUSE THE COMIC BOOK LIBRARY, WAS READY TO OPEN.
THEY CHARGED EACH CHILD 10 CENTS ADMISSION TO THE LIBRARY, WHICH WAS OPEN FOR TWO HOURS EVERY DAY AFTER SCHOOL.
THE CUSTOMERS WOULD READ AS MANY COMICS AS THEY COULD IN TWO HOURS.
IT WAS A BARGAIN FOR THEM, SINCE A COMIC COST 10 CENTS EACH, AND THEY COULD READ FIVE OR SIX IN TWO HOURS.

MIKE AND ROBERT AVERAGED $9.50 PER WEEK OVER A THREE-MONTH PERIOD. THEY PAID MIKE'S SISTER $1 A WEEK TO WATCH THE LIBRARY WHEN THEY WEREN'T AROUND.
THEY KEPT THEIR AGREEMENT WITH RICH DAD AND MRS. MARTIN BY WORKING IN THE STORE EVERY SATURDAY.
THEY ALSO KEPT THEIR AGREEMENT TO THE DISTRIBUTOR BY NOT SELLING ANY COMIC BOOKS.
MIKE'S DAD WAS EXCITED BECAUSE THEY HAD LEARNED THE FIRST LESSON SO WELL. HE HAD NEW THINGS HE COULD BEGIN TO TEACH THEM NOW.
BY NOT GETTING PAID TO WORK AT THE STORE, THEY WERE FORCED TO USE THEIR IMAGINATIONS TO SPOT AN OPPORTUNITY TO MAKE MONEY. BY STARTING THEIR OWN BUSINESS, THEY HAD TAKEN CONTROL OF THEIR OWN FINANCES, AND WERE NO LONGER DEPENDENT ON AN EMPLOYER.
INSTEAD OF PAYING THEM MONEY, MIKE'S DAD HAD GIVEN THEM MUCH MORE.

4

Opportunities Are Everywhere

Tina

OK, THAT'S A REALLY GREAT STORY... BUT WHAT DOES IT HAVE TO DO WITH ME?
I MEAN, IT'S NOT LIKE YOU CAN EVEN GET COMIC BOOKS ON A NEWSSTAND ANYMORE, MUCH LESS MAKE MONEY OFF OF THEM. AND WITH MOVIE AND VIDEO GAME RENTALS, THERE'S NO WAY ANYONE'S GONNA PAY TO "RENT" A COMIC BOOK.
WELL, YEAH, YOU'RE RIGHT. IT WOULDN'T WORK TODAY. BUT THAT'S NOT THE POINT.
THE POINT IS, EVEN WHEN HE WAS A KID, ROBERT DIDN'T START FINDING THE OPPORTUNITIES UNTIL HE OPENED HIS MIND AND STARTED LOOKING.
LEMONADE
IT'S NOT LIKE HE'S THE ONLY ONE, EITHER. LOTS OF KIDS OUT THERE HAVE FOUND THEIR OWN OPPORTUNITIES.
THAT'S WHAT YOU NEED TO KEEP AN EYE OUT FOR...
IF YOU WANT TO BECOME RICH.

OKAY... SO DID THIS WHOLE "OPPORTUNITIES" THING WORK FOR *YOU?*
WELL, I'M NOT RICH YET, IF THAT'S WHAT YOU'RE ASKING...
BUT I'M *WORKING* ON IT.
AFTER I READ THAT STORY, I FIGURED THERE WAS A LOT MORE THAT I NEEDED TO LEARN.
SO I SPENT A LOT OF TIME LOOKING AROUND FOR IDEAS ABOUT HOW TO MAKE MONEY AND DOING THINGS LIKE READING BOOKS, GOING TO WEBSITES, STUFF LIKE THAT.
INVESTING FOR THE BEGINNER
DOLLARS
I LEARNED PRETTY FAST THAT IF I REALLY WANTED TO GET RICH, DOING THINGS LIKE MOWING LAWNS AND MY PAPER ROUTE WEREN'T GOING TO DO IT.
SO, I STARTED LOOKING AROUND TO SEE IF I COULD FIND AN OPPORTUNITY FOR MYSELF.
AFTER A WHILE, I HAD AN IDEA.

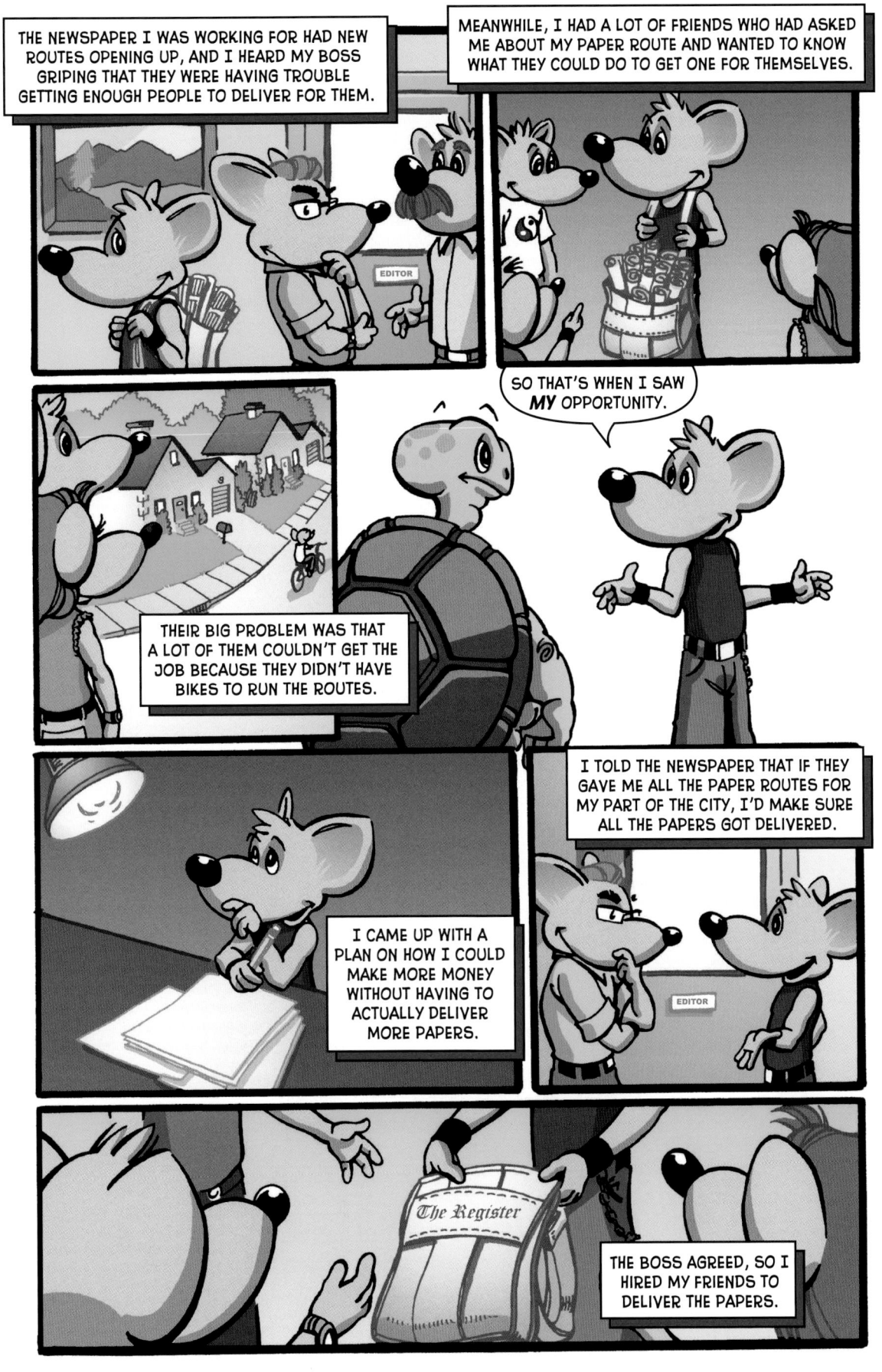
THE NEWSPAPER I WAS WORKING FOR HAD NEW ROUTES OPENING UP, AND I HEARD MY BOSS GRIPING THAT THEY WERE HAVING TROUBLE GETTING ENOUGH PEOPLE TO DELIVER FOR THEM.
EDITOR
MEANWHILE, I HAD A LOT OF FRIENDS WHO HAD ASKED ME ABOUT MY PAPER ROUTE AND WANTED TO KNOW WHAT THEY COULD DO TO GET ONE FOR THEMSELVES.
SO THAT'S WHEN I SAW MY OPPORTUNITY.
THEIR BIG PROBLEM WAS THAT A LOT OF THEM COULDN'T GET THE JOB BECAUSE THEY DIDN'T HAVE BIKES TO RUN THE ROUTES.
I CAME UP WITH A PLAN ON HOW I COULD MAKE MORE MONEY WITHOUT HAVING TO ACTUALLY DELIVER MORE PAPERS.
I TOLD THE NEWSPAPER THAT IF THEY GAVE ME ALL THE PAPER ROUTES FOR MY PART OF THE CITY, I'D MAKE SURE ALL THE PAPERS GOT DELIVERED.
EDITOR
The Register
THE BOSS AGREED, SO I HIRED MY FRIENDS TO DELIVER THE PAPERS.

MY MOM AND DAD HAD A COUPLE OF OLD BIKES THAT THEY DIDN'T USE ANYMORE AND I HAD A BIKE I WANTED TO REPLACE. MY FRIENDS WHO DIDN'T HAVE BIKES COULD RENT THEM FROM ME TO MAKE THEIR DELIVERIES.
MY FRIENDS WERE HAPPY BECAUSE THEY GOT THE PAPER ROUTES THEY WANTED.
AND THE NEWSPAPER WAS HAPPY BECAUSE IT DIDN'T NEED TO WORRY ABOUT GETTING THE PAPERS DELIVERED.
EDITOR
BEFORE LONG, NOT ONLY DID I HAVE MY NEW BIKE, BUT I STILL HAD MONEY COMING IN FROM THE BIKE RENTALS!
WOW! I GUESS THERE'S A LOT I NEED TO LEARN ABOUT MONEY...
WHERE DO I START?

WELL, THE FIRST THING I HAD TO LEARN WAS HOW TO READ A FINANCIAL STATEMENT.
A FINANCIAL STATEMENT? WHAT'S THAT?
YOU CAN'T BUILD A SKYSCRAPER WITHOUT A GOOD BLUEPRINT, RIGHT? BUILDING MONEY IS LIKE THAT. YOU NEED TO HAVE A GOOD BLUEPRINT.
THAT'S KIND OF WHAT A FINANCIAL STATEMENT IS.
ONCE YOU LEARN HOW TO READ ONE, YOU CAN FIND OUT WHERE ALL YOUR MONEY IS GOING, AND HOW TO MAKE MORE OF IT.
THIS TOP PART IS CALLED AN INCOME STATEMENT. SOME PEOPLE CALL IT A PROFIT AND LOSS STATEMENT BECAUSE IT SHOWS ALL YOUR INCOME COMING IN AND YOUR EXPENSES GOING OUT. AND WHAT IS LEFT IS YOUR CASH FLOW.
INCOME
SALARY
DIVIDENDS
EXPENSES
RENT
ELECTRICITY
CREDIT CARD PAYMENT
FOOD
LIABILITIES
CAR LOAN
HOUSE MORTGAGE
CREDIT CARD
ASSETS
PROPERTY
INVESTMENTS
SAVINGS ACCOUNTS
BUSINESSES
DOWN THERE TOWARDS THE BOTTOM, THAT PART IS THE BALANCE SHEET. IT SHOWS YOUR ASSETS AND LIABILITIES.
AND ONCE YOU KNOW HOW THEY WORK TOGETHER, YOU'LL BE ABLE TO SEE HOW YOUR MONEY FLOWS BETWEEN THEM. IT'S PRETTY EASY TO GET THE HANG OF.

TAKE THIS PART, THE INCOME STATEMENT. IT TRACKS ALL THE MONEY YOU MAKE...
AND THE MONEY YOU SPEND... EVERY MONTH.
FOR MOST PEOPLE, THE MONEY THEY MAKE GETS SUCKED AWAY BY THEIR EXPENSES.
BUT WHEN YOU HAVE MORE INCOME THAN EXPENSES THE REMAINING INCOME IS CALLED CASH FLOW. THAT'S THE KIND OF MONEY YOU WANT! IT'S THE AMOUNT OF MONEY YOU HAVE AT THE END OF THE MONTH.
FOOD
CASHFLOW
ASSETS
PROPERTY

THE BOTTOM SECTION IS CALLED A BALANCE SHEET. THAT'S BECAUSE IT LISTS YOUR ASSETS AND LIABILITIES.
...IF YOU ARE DOING THINGS RIGHT!
UM, ASSETS? LIABILITIES?
DIVIDENDS
EXPENSES
RENT
ELECTRICITY
CREDIT CARD PAYMENT
FOOD
ASSETS
LIABILITIES
OH, SORRY, MAN... ASSETS ARE THINGS THAT PUT MONEY IN YOUR POCKET.
SO, IF YOU BUY AN ASSET IT MAKES MORE INCOME AND RESULTS IN A CASH FLOW PATTERN LIKE THIS...
PROPERTY
INVESTMENTS
OK, I GET THAT PART BUT, LIKE, WHAT KINDS OF THINGS ARE ASSETS?
ASSETS
STOCK ISSUE
SMOOTHIES
WELL, ASSETS CAN BE STUFF LIKE SAVINGS ACCOUNTS, BUSINESSES, OR EVEN AN APARTMENT COMPLEX OR PROPERTY THAT YOU OWN LIKE THE BICYCLES THAT I RENTED TO MY FRIENDS. IF IT GIVES YOU MONEY WITHOUT YOU WORKING, THEN IT'S AN ASSET.

NOW, ***LIABILITIES*** ON THE OTHER HAND... THOSE ARE THINGS LIKE MORTGAGES, MAGAZINE SUBSCRIPTIONS, CAR LOANS...
...OR CREDIT CARD BALANCES.
WHEN YOU SPEND MONEY ON LIABILITIES, THAT MONEY IS GONE. YOU'LL NEVER SEE ANOTHER CENT OF IT.
LIABILTIES CREATE A CASH FLOW PATTERN LIKE THIS.
EXPENSES
LIABILITIES
THEY TAKE MONEY OUT OF YOUR POCKET.

ONCE YOU UNDERSTAND HOW ASSETS AND LIABILITIES WORK YOU CAN TELL REALLY QUICKLY IF SOMEONE IS ***ACTUALLY*** RICH OR NOT.
DUDE, IF SOMEONE'S RICH, THEY'RE RICH. IT'S NOT LIKE THERE'S A LOT OF ROOM FOR DOUBT!
WELL, THERE IS ACTUALLY. TO TELL IF PEOPLE ARE ***REALLY*** RICH, AND NOT JUST ***LOOKING*** RICH...
ALL YOU HAVE TO DO IS LOOK AT THE THINGS THEY SPEND THEIR MONEY ON, AND WHAT THEIR CASH FLOW PATTERN LOOKS LIKE.
INCOME
ASSETS
LIKE, WHEN PEOPLE ARE JUST STARTING OUT IN LIFE, THEIR CASH FLOW PATTERN LOOKS LIKE THIS. SINCE THEY DON'T HAVE MANY ASSETS OR LIABILITIES, THEIR JOBS BRING MONEY IN AND PAY FOR THEIR EXPENSES.
BUT, ONCE THEY START TO BRING IN MORE MONEY, THEY GO OUT AND BUY NEW HOUSES AND CARS.
LIABILITIES
CAR LOAN
HOUSE MORTGAGE
THEN, THEIR PATTERN ENDS UP LOOKING LIKE THIS.
ASSETS
LOAN
MORTGAGE
SURE, THEY'RE MAKING MORE MONEY, BUT WITH THE EXTRA DOUGH, ALL THEY'VE BOUGHT IS MORE LIABILITIES, WHICH'LL JUST SUCK THEIR MONTHLY CASH FLOW DOWN TO NOTHING ***REAL*** FAST.

OK, WAIT, SO LET ME GET THIS STRAIGHT... A BETTER PLAN WOULD BE TO SPEND MY MONEY ON ASSETS, RIGHT?
'CAUSE THE ASSETS WILL MAKE ME MORE MONEY...
...WHICH MEANS MONEY IN MY POCKET AND I GET RICH!
RIGHT. IF YOU WANT TO BECOME RICH, JUST BUY ASSETS INSTEAD OF LIABILITIES.
SO ASSETS ARE LIKE MONEY GROWING ON TREES.

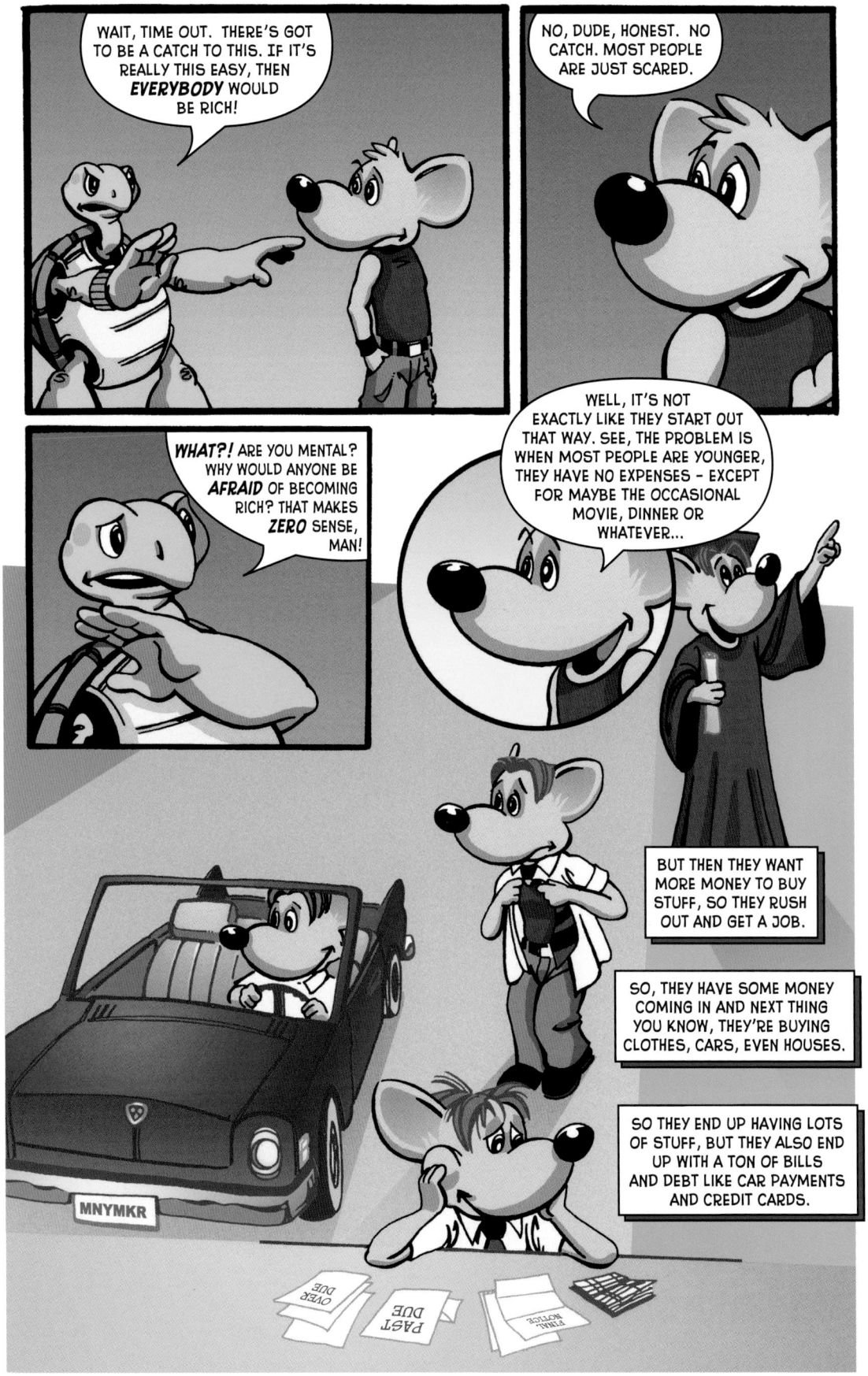
WAIT, TIME OUT. THERE'S GOT TO BE A CATCH TO THIS. IF IT'S REALLY THIS EASY, THEN EVERYBODY WOULD BE RICH!
NO, DUDE, HONEST. NO CATCH. MOST PEOPLE ARE JUST SCARED.
WHAT?! ARE YOU MENTAL? WHY WOULD ANYONE BE AFRAID OF BECOMING RICH? THAT MAKES ZERO SENSE, MAN!
WELL, IT'S NOT EXACTLY LIKE THEY START OUT THAT WAY. SEE, THE PROBLEM IS WHEN MOST PEOPLE ARE YOUNGER, THEY HAVE NO EXPENSES - EXCEPT FOR MAYBE THE OCCASIONAL MOVIE, DINNER OR WHATEVER...
BUT THEN THEY WANT MORE MONEY TO BUY STUFF, SO THEY RUSH OUT AND GET A JOB.
SO, THEY HAVE SOME MONEY COMING IN AND NEXT THING YOU KNOW, THEY'RE BUYING CLOTHES, CARS, EVEN HOUSES.
SO THEY END UP HAVING LOTS OF STUFF, BUT THEY ALSO END UP WITH A TON OF BILLS AND DEBT LIKE CAR PAYMENTS AND CREDIT CARDS.
MNYMKR
OVER DUE
PAST DUE
FINAL NOTICE

THEY WORK LIKE CRAZY BECAUSE THEY KNOW IF THEY DON'T PAY THEIR BILLS, THEY'LL LOSE ALL THE EXPENSIVE STUFF THEY'VE BOUGHT.
SO WHEN THEY ACTUALLY CAN SAVE UP SOME EXTRA MONEY, THEY'RE FREAKED OUT ABOUT DOING ANYTHING WITH IT. THEY'RE SCARED THEY MIGHT LOSE THEIR JOBS AND THAT MEANS THEY CAN'T PAY THOSE BILLS...
SO THEY GET STUCK IN THAT TRAP: SCARED TO DEATH, WORKING LIKE CRAZY, AND NEVER GETTING AHEAD. THAT'S CALLED THE RAT RACE.
NOW, I'M NOT SAYING THERE'S ANYTHING WRONG WITH HAVING A JOB.
I WAS ABOUT TO SAY...
EVERYONE NEEDS SOME WAY OF GETTING STARTED, AND A JOB IS ONE WAY TO MAKE MONEY AND A GREAT WAY TO LEARN ABOUT A FIELD THAT INTERESTS YOU.
HOT DOGS
HELP WANTED
BUT THAT JOB'S NOT GONNA MAKE YOU RICH. IT'S THE THINGS THAT YOU DO, LIKE BUYING ASSETS AND NOT RACKING UP A BUNCH OF CREDIT CARD BILLS, THAT'LL MAKE YOU RICH.

WAIT, BUT LET'S SAY I GET SOME SWEET JOB THAT PAYS HUGE AMOUNTS OF CASH... CAN'T I GET RICH LIKE THAT?
SOME FOLKS THINK YOU CAN, BUT THEY'RE KINDA FOOLIN' THEMSELVES INTO THINKING THEY'RE RICH BECAUSE THEY HAVE A FANCY CAR, OR BECAUSE THEY HAVE A FAT PAYCHECK.
BUT, NEWSFLASH DUDE... HAVING THE SWEET WHEELS, OR EVEN HAVING COLD HARD CASH, DOESN'T MEAN YOU'RE RICH.
OK, WAIT, YOU LOST ME AGAIN...
OK, LET'S LOOK AT IT THIS WAY. EVEN IF YOU HAVE A GREAT JOB THAT PAYS YOU A LOT OF MONEY, WHAT HAPPENS IF YOU LOSE YOUR JOB?
WELL, SINCE I'M NOT WORKING, THERE'S NO PAYCHECK, WHICH MEANS I HAVE NO MONEY COMING IN, SO MY CASH FLOW GETS NAILED, RIGHT?
EXACTLY. SINCE ALL YOUR MONEY'S COMING FROM A JOB, YOU'RE STILL AT ITS MERCY. AND IF YOUR JOB GOES AWAY...
INCOME
DANGER
NONE
NADA
NOPE, NO CASH!
EXPENSES
RENT
ELECTRICITY
CREDIT CARD
FOOD

JUST SPIT IT OUT, MAN. WHAT IS IT THAT MAKES YOU "RICH" OR NOT?
WELL, TURN THE SITUATION AROUND FOR A SECOND. WHAT WOULD HAPPEN IF YOU HAD ASSETS THAT BROUGHT IN ENOUGH MONEY TO PAY FOR EVERYTHING?
HMMM... I GUESS IN THAT CASE, IT WOULDN'T MATTER WHETHER I LOST MY JOB OR NOT 'CAUSE I'D STILL HAVE MY ASSETS BRINGING MONEY IN, RIGHT?
INCOME
SALARY
DIVIDENDS
RENT
PROPERTY
INVESTMENTS
SAVINGS ACCOUNTS
BUSINESSES
EXACTLY. IF YOU DO THAT, YOU NEVER HAVE TO WORK AGAIN IN ORDER TO TAKE CARE OF THINGS, AND THAT'S WHAT BEING RICH IS.
THE REALLY COOL PART OF IT IS THAT, WHEN IT COMES TO GETTING RICH, WE'VE ACTUALLY GOT AN ADVANTAGE OVER MOST GROWN-UPS.
WHAT?! HELLO--I DON'T MAKE ANY MONEY! THAT'S WHY I HAD TO SIT OUT GOING ON THE "ELIMINATOR," REMEMBER?
YEAH, TRUE. BUT, YOU DON'T HAVE A TRUCKLOAD OF EXPENSES AND LIABILITIES EITHER.
YOU AND I CAN WORK TO SCORE SOME EXTRA MONEY TO BUY STUFF, BUT WE DON'T NEED TO HAVE A JOB. SO, IF WE WATCH IT NOW, AND BUILD UP ASSETS, BY THE TIME WE'RE OLDER WE WON'T HAVE A LOT OF THE EXPENSES AND LIABILITIES TO KEEP US FROM BEING WAY RICH!
REAL ESTATE
BUSINESSES
BONDS
RENTALS
PROPERTY
CASH
OPTIONS
DEBTS
EXPENSES
BILLS

5

Let's Do It!

LET'S DO IT!

OK, SO HOW DO I GET STARTED THEN?
WELL, EACH TIME YOU GET ANY MONEY, DON'T BLOW IT ALL IMMEDIATELY.
TAKE SOME OF IT, AND PUT IT AWAY.
PART OF WHAT YOU PUT ASIDE SHOULD BE FOR SAVINGS.
SOME OF IT'S FOR INVESTING.
AND SOME SHOULD GO TO CHARITY.
SAVINGS
CDs
Bonds
Accounts
INVESTING
Businesses
Stocks
CHARITY
Afterschool Programs
Medical Research
Church
Homeless Shelters
SAVINGS
INVESTING
Businesses
IF YOU DO THIS EVERY TIME YOU GET MONEY, AFTER A WHILE, YOUR SAVINGS WILL GIVE YOU THE FUNDS THAT YOU'LL NEED IN ORDER TO BUY ASSETS LATER.

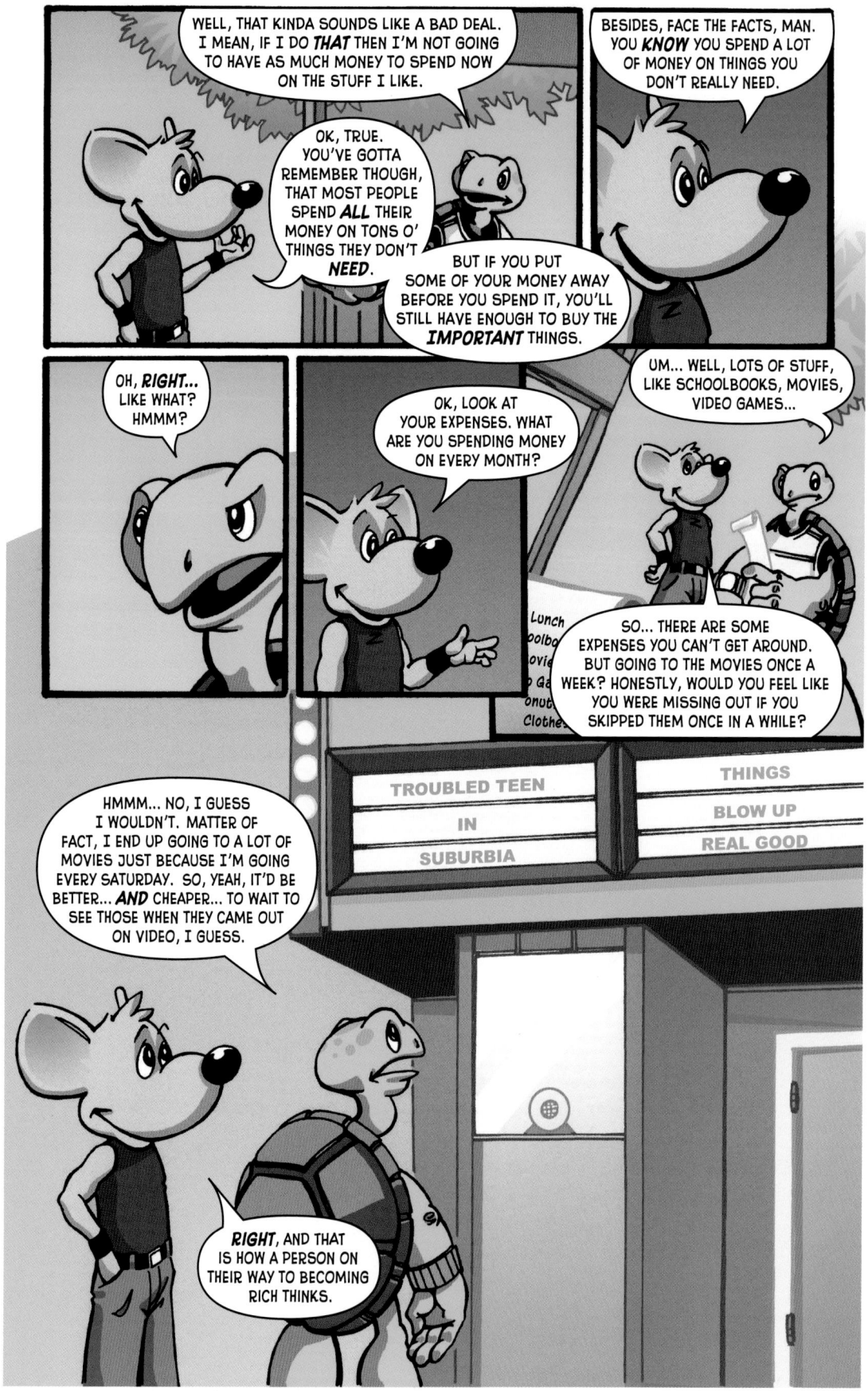
WELL, THAT KINDA SOUNDS LIKE A BAD DEAL. I MEAN, IF I DO THAT THEN I'M NOT GOING TO HAVE AS MUCH MONEY TO SPEND NOW ON THE STUFF I LIKE.
OK, TRUE. YOU'VE GOTTA REMEMBER THOUGH, THAT MOST PEOPLE SPEND ALL THEIR MONEY ON TONS O' THINGS THEY DON'T NEED.
BUT IF YOU PUT SOME OF YOUR MONEY AWAY BEFORE YOU SPEND IT, YOU'LL STILL HAVE ENOUGH TO BUY THE IMPORTANT THINGS.
BESIDES, FACE THE FACTS, MAN. YOU KNOW YOU SPEND A LOT OF MONEY ON THINGS YOU DON'T REALLY NEED.
OH, RIGHT... LIKE WHAT? HMMM?
OK, LOOK AT YOUR EXPENSES. WHAT ARE YOU SPENDING MONEY ON EVERY MONTH?
UM... WELL, LOTS OF STUFF, LIKE SCHOOLBOOKS, MOVIES, VIDEO GAMES...
SO... THERE ARE SOME EXPENSES YOU CAN'T GET AROUND. BUT GOING TO THE MOVIES ONCE A WEEK? HONESTLY, WOULD YOU FEEL LIKE YOU WERE MISSING OUT IF YOU SKIPPED THEM ONCE IN A WHILE?
TROUBLED TEEN
IN
SUBURBIA
THINGS
BLOW UP
REAL GOOD
HMMM... NO, I GUESS I WOULDN'T. MATTER OF FACT, I END UP GOING TO A LOT OF MOVIES JUST BECAUSE I'M GOING EVERY SATURDAY. SO, YEAH, IT'D BE BETTER... AND CHEAPER... TO WAIT TO SEE THOSE WHEN THEY CAME OUT ON VIDEO, I GUESS.
RIGHT, AND THAT IS HOW A PERSON ON THEIR WAY TO BECOMING RICH THINKS.

WELL, THAT'S EASY ENOUGH. BUT EVEN IF SKIPPING A MOVIE ONCE IN A WHILE SAVES ME MONEY, THERE'S NO WAY THAT JUST DOING THAT IS GOING TO MAKE ME RICH.
NOT BY ITSELF. BUT SAVING MONEY AND STARTING TO INVEST IS A GREAT WAY TO GET STARTED.
OK, SAY I GET ENOUGH MONEY STASHED AWAY. HOW DO I FIGURE OUT WHAT KINDS OF ASSETS TO BUY?
INVESTING
Businesses
Stocks
WELL, ONE OF THE IMPORTANT THINGS TO REMEMBER IS THAT YOU NEED TO BUY THE TYPES OF ASSETS YOU'RE INTERESTED IN. IF YOU DO THAT, YOU'LL BE ABLE TO MAKE BETTER CHOICES, BECAUSE YOU UNDERSTAND THOSE THINGS BETTER.
SOME EXAMPLES OF THE TYPES OF THINGS THAT YOU CAN INVEST IN ARE STOCKS, REAL ESTATE, OR YOU COULD START YOUR OWN BUSINESS.
LEMONADE
PUBLIC ISSUE OF STOCK
100 Shares
WHAT YOU BUY DOESN'T REALLY MATTER. AS LONG AS IT PAYS YOU MONEY EVERY MONTH, WITHOUT YOU HAVING TO WORK AT A JOB FOR IT.

OK, WELL THAT'S ALL FINE AND GOOD DUDE, BUT I'M JUST A BIT TOO YOUNG TO BUY THE KINDS OF ASSETS YOU WERE TALKING ABOUT. AND I DON'T THINK MY DAD IS ABOUT TO BUY AN APARTMENT COMPLEX FOR ME TO RENT!
I KNOW IT MAY SEEM LIKE THAT, BUT SERIOUSLY, AGE DOESN'T REALLY MATTER ALL THAT MUCH. THE KEY IS YOU HAVE TO ALWAYS BE LOOKING FOR THE OPPORTUNITIES AND POTENTIAL ASSETS THAT MOST PEOPLE DON'T SEE.
ONCE YOU START LOOKING, YOU'LL SEE OPPORTUNITIES EVERYWHERE.
MATTER OF FACT, YOU'LL EVEN FIND THAT SOME OPPORTUNITIES ARE EASIER TO FIND FOR KIDS.
OH SURE, LIKE WHAT?
APARTMENTS
TAXI
MAGAZINES
DATASOFT
U-STORE-IT

OK, LOOK AT WHAT ROBERT DID FOR EXAMPLE... MOST ADULTS WOULD HAVE MISSED THAT OPPORTUNITY ENTIRELY.
BUT BECAUSE HE WAS A KID HE KNEW WHAT THE OTHER KIDS WOULD BE INTERESTED IN. SO HE WAS ABLE TO SEE AN OPPORTUNITY RENTING OUT THE COMIC BOOKS.
YEAH, I SUPPOSE HE DID FIND SOMETHING THAT OTHER ADULTS WOULD HAVE MISSED.
EXACTLY...
BUT HE NEVER WOULD HAVE DONE THAT IF HE HADN'T BEEN LOOKING FOR THE OPPORTUNITIES.

SO WHAT ELSE HAVE KIDS FOUND?
WELL, HOW ABOUT THE COLLECTIBLE CARD GAMES?
WHEN THOSE CAME OUT MOST CARDS CAME IN PACKS THAT YOU COULD BUY FOR A FEW DOLLARS, BUT THERE WERE RARE ONES SCATTERED HERE AND THERE THAT COULD BE WORTH A LOT OF MONEY. SO A LOT OF THE FANS STARTED BUYING AND SELLING CARDS.
PRETTY SOON THEY HAD SMALL CARD STANDS SET UP AT THE LOCAL TOURNAMENTS WHERE OTHER KIDS COULD SELL THEIR CARDS FOR THEM.
A LOT OF THEM EVEN STARTED PUTTING UP WEB PAGES AND SELLING THE CARDS OVER THE INTERNET.
YEAH, I CAN SEE THAT - BUT DUDE, COMICS AND COLLECTOR CARDS ARE PRETTY MUCH DEAD...
THAT'S TRUE... MAYBE THE SAME KIND OF MONEY CAN'T BE MADE THERE TODAY. BUT THE IDEA IS THAT BY KEEPING YOUR EYES OPEN YOU CAN SEE NEW OPPORTUNITIES.
WHO KNOWS WHAT THE NEXT HOT ITEM WILL BE?
I GUESS YOU'RE RIGHT ... I MEAN, SOMEONE HAS TO DISCOVER IT ...
...AND THERE'S NO REASON IT CAN'T BE YOU!
THE POINT IS, YOU HAVE TO START LOOKING FOR THOSE OPPORTUNITIES NOW! JUST BECAUSE YOU'RE YOUNG DOESN'T MEAN THAT YOU CAN'T FIND THEM.

OR, FOR EXAMPLE, YOU CAN TRY TO START YOUR OWN BUSINESS.
WAIT A SEC... YOU WERE STARTING TO MAKE SENSE, BUT THERE'S JUST NO WAY I CAN START A BUSINESS.

DUDE, SURE YOU CAN. LOTS OF KIDS OUT THERE HAVE DONE IT.
AND MANY OF THOSE BUSINESSES HAVE BEEN WAY SUCCESSFUL BECAUSE KIDS KNOW BETTER THAN ANYONE WHAT OTHER KIDS WANT.

OK, LET'S JUST PRETEND THAT YOU'RE RIGHT. JUST WHAT IS IT THAT I'M SUPPOSED TO START A BUSINESS IN?

WHAT YOU DECIDE TO DO ISN'T AS IMPORTANT AS MAKING SURE YOU'RE ALWAYS LOOKING FOR OPPORTUNITIES.

IF YOU'RE LOOKING AT THINGS THAT YOU'RE EXCITED ABOUT, YOU'RE A LOT MORE LIKELY TO FIND AN OPPORTUNITY THERE BEFORE ANYONE ELSE.

EVEN BETTER, WE HAVE A HUGE ADVANTAGE OVER ADULTS.
AT OUR AGE, WE'VE GOT IT MADE. WE'VE GOT PLENTY OF TIME TO MAKE MISTAKES AND LEARN FROM THEM WITHOUT IT HURTING OUR FUTURE TOO MUCH.
SEE, THE LATER YOU START, THE HARDER IT IS TO GET GOING. THAT'S BECAUSE WHEN YOU GET TO OUR PARENTS' AGE, YOU'VE GOT THAT STEAMER TRUNK OF BAGGAGE STRAPPED TO YOUR BACK.
BUT, AT OUR AGE, YOU DON'T HAVE ALL THAT STUFF LIKE RENT, PHONE BILLS, CAR INSURANCE, OR THE MILLIONS OF OTHER THINGS IN LIFE THAT END UP FILLING UP THAT LIABILITIES COLUMN.
SO, IF YOU CAN GET YOUR ASSET COLUMN BUILT UP BEFORE YOU EVER START GETTING THINGS IN THE LIABILITIES COLUMN...THEN THE MOMENTUM WORKS TO YOUR FAVOR.
ASSETS

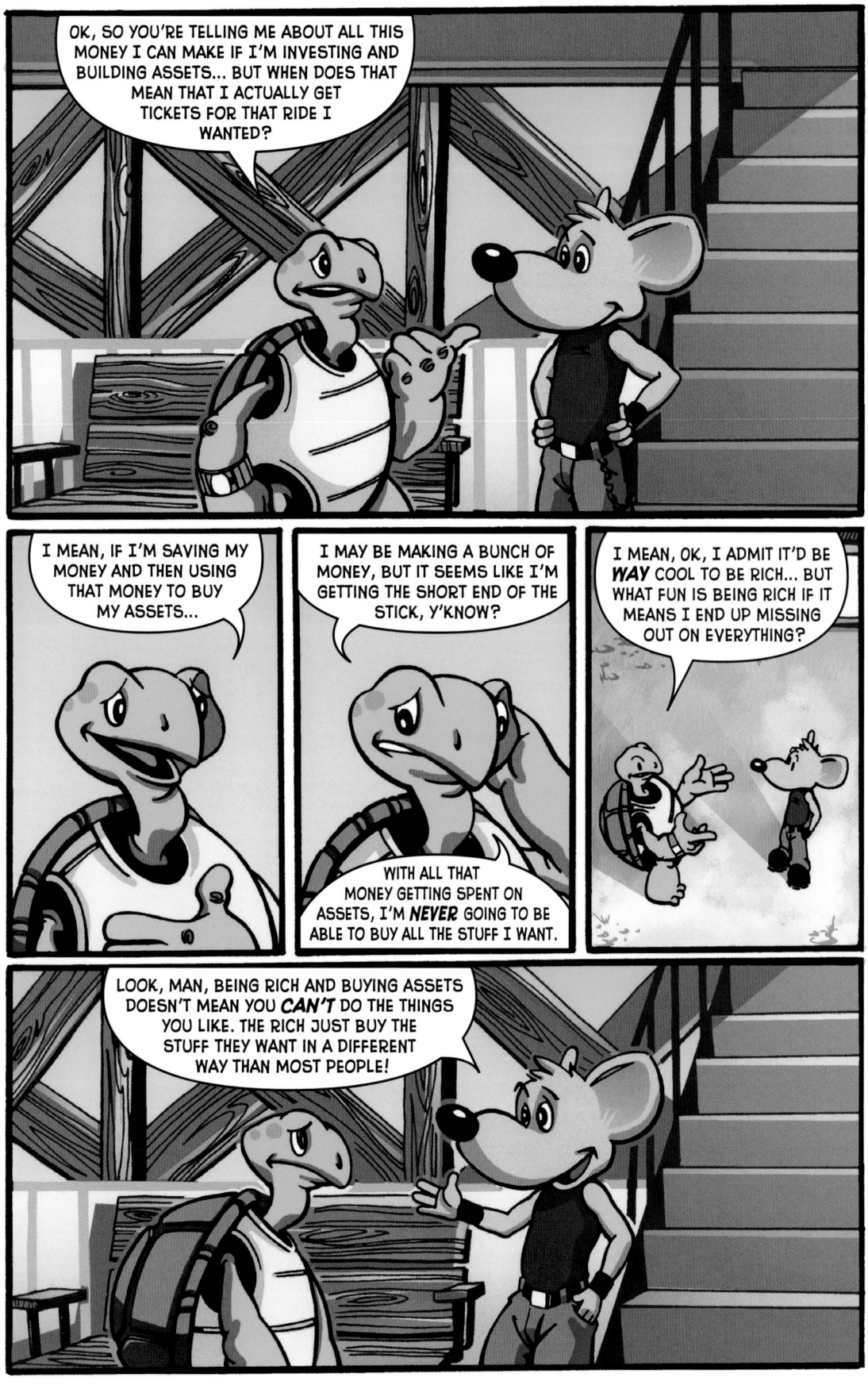
OK, SO YOU'RE TELLING ME ABOUT ALL THIS MONEY I CAN MAKE IF I'M INVESTING AND BUILDING ASSETS... BUT WHEN DOES THAT MEAN THAT I ACTUALLY GET TICKETS FOR THAT RIDE I WANTED?
I MEAN, IF I'M SAVING MY MONEY AND THEN USING THAT MONEY TO BUY MY ASSETS...
I MAY BE MAKING A BUNCH OF MONEY, BUT IT SEEMS LIKE I'M GETTING THE SHORT END OF THE STICK, Y'KNOW?
WITH ALL THAT MONEY GETTING SPENT ON ASSETS, I'M NEVER GOING TO BE ABLE TO BUY ALL THE STUFF I WANT.
I MEAN, OK, I ADMIT IT'D BE WAY COOL TO BE RICH... BUT WHAT FUN IS BEING RICH IF IT MEANS I END UP MISSING OUT ON EVERYTHING?
LOOK, MAN, BEING RICH AND BUYING ASSETS DOESN'T MEAN YOU CAN'T DO THE THINGS YOU LIKE. THE RICH JUST BUY THE STUFF THEY WANT IN A DIFFERENT WAY THAN MOST PEOPLE!

FOR INSTANCE, WHEN MOST PEOPLE WANT SOMETHING THEY USUALLY JUST GO OUT AND BUY IT. AND A LOT OF TIMES, WHEN THEY DON'T HAVE ENOUGH CASH THEY PUT IT ON CREDIT CARDS.
TICKETS
HOTDOGS
ATM
BUT THAT'S NOT THINKING THE WAY YOU HAVE TO IF YOU WANT TO BE RICH. ALL THAT LEAVES YOU WITH IS THE STUFF YOU WANTED BADLY AT THAT MOMENT- AND NO MONEY.
TICKETS
HOTDOGS
ATM
THAT STUFF'LL BREAK OR WEAR OUT OVER TIME AND THEN COST YOU MORE MONEY TO GET NEW STUFF TO REPLACE IT. THAT'S THE THING: IT COSTS YOU MONEY, INSTEAD OF GIVING YOU MONEY.
TICKETS
HOTDOGS
ATM
LOOK AT HOW THE RICH DO IT.
INSTEAD OF JUST RUNNING OUT AND BUYING WHAT THEY WANT, THEY USE THAT MONEY TO BUILD ASSETS INSTEAD.
THEN THEY MAKE THE ASSET GROW AND USE ITS PROFITS TO BUY WHATEVER IT WAS THEY WANTED.
BY INVESTING IN ASSETS, YOU ALWAYS HAVE CASH COMING AT YOU, TO SPEND HOWEVER YOU WANT, ALL WITHOUT WORKING AT A JOB.

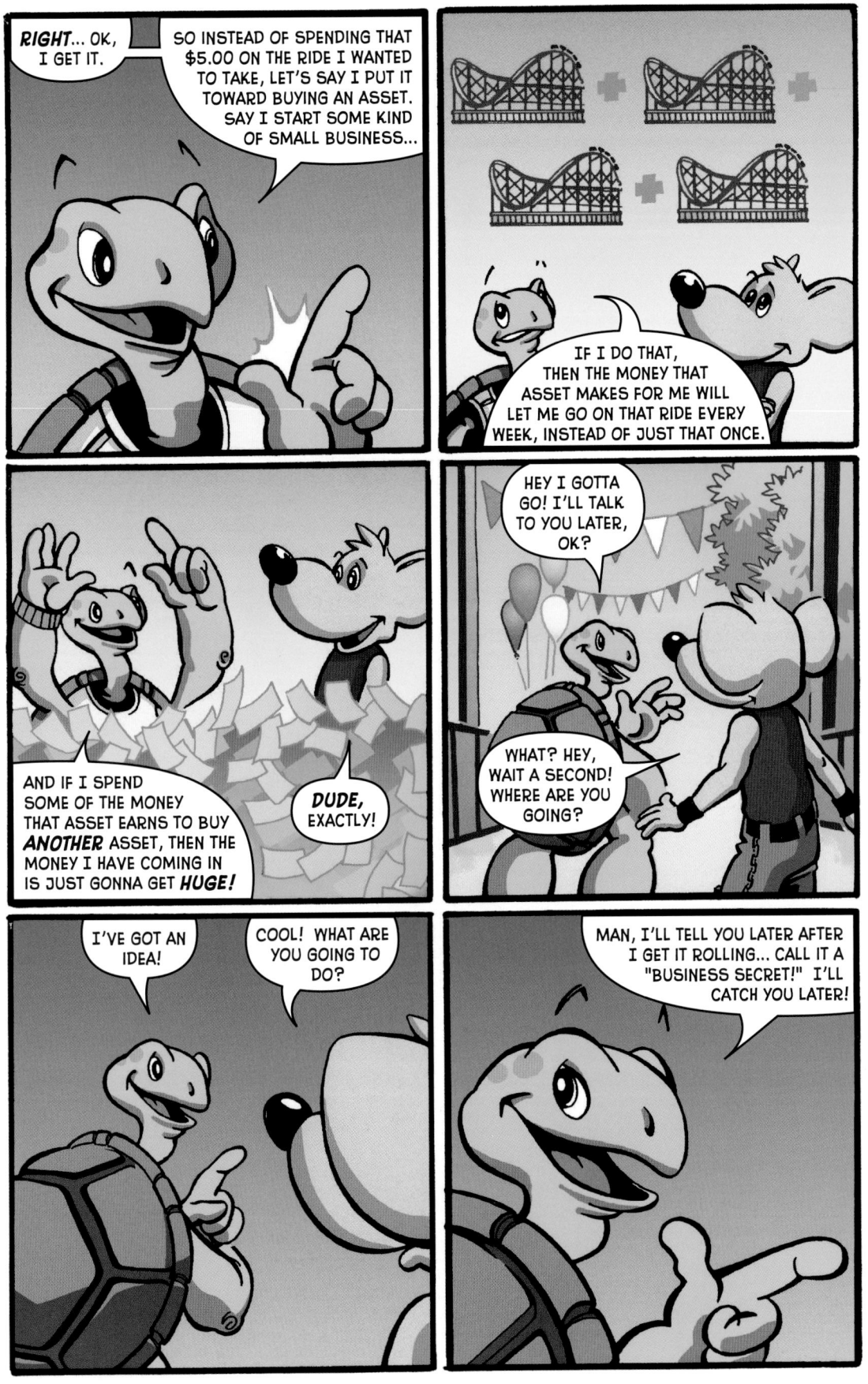
RIGHT... OK, I GET IT.
SO INSTEAD OF SPENDING THAT $5.00 ON THE RIDE I WANTED TO TAKE, LET'S SAY I PUT IT TOWARD BUYING AN ASSET. SAY I START SOME KIND OF SMALL BUSINESS...
IF I DO THAT, THEN THE MONEY THAT ASSET MAKES FOR ME WILL LET ME GO ON THAT RIDE EVERY WEEK, INSTEAD OF JUST THAT ONCE.
AND IF I SPEND SOME OF THE MONEY THAT ASSET EARNS TO BUY ANOTHER ASSET, THEN THE MONEY I HAVE COMING IN IS JUST GONNA GET HUGE!
DUDE, EXACTLY!
HEY I GOTTA GO! I'LL TALK TO YOU LATER, OK?
WHAT? HEY, WAIT A SECOND! WHERE ARE YOU GOING?
I'VE GOT AN IDEA!
COOL! WHAT ARE YOU GOING TO DO?
MAN, I'LL TELL YOU LATER AFTER I GET IT ROLLING... CALL IT A "BUSINESS SECRET!" I'LL CATCH YOU LATER!

ONE MONTH LATER
BUMPER CARS
UNDER NEW MANAGE
Same great taste!
TIM! WHATS UP? I HAVEN'T SEEN YOU IN WEEKS, MAN!
HEY RED, SORRY GUY, BEEN BUSY!
IT'S COOL. SO, HOW'VE THINGS BEEN GOING?
IT'S BEEN SWEET, MAN! TALKING TO YOU REALLY GOT ME THINKING.
SO, I KEPT THINKING ABOUT A JOB NOT GETTING ME THE MONEY I'D NEED TO BE RICH.
RICH?
YEAH-, SO I DECIDED TO START MY OWN BUSINESS.
WAIT A SEC... YOU STARTED A BUSINESS?

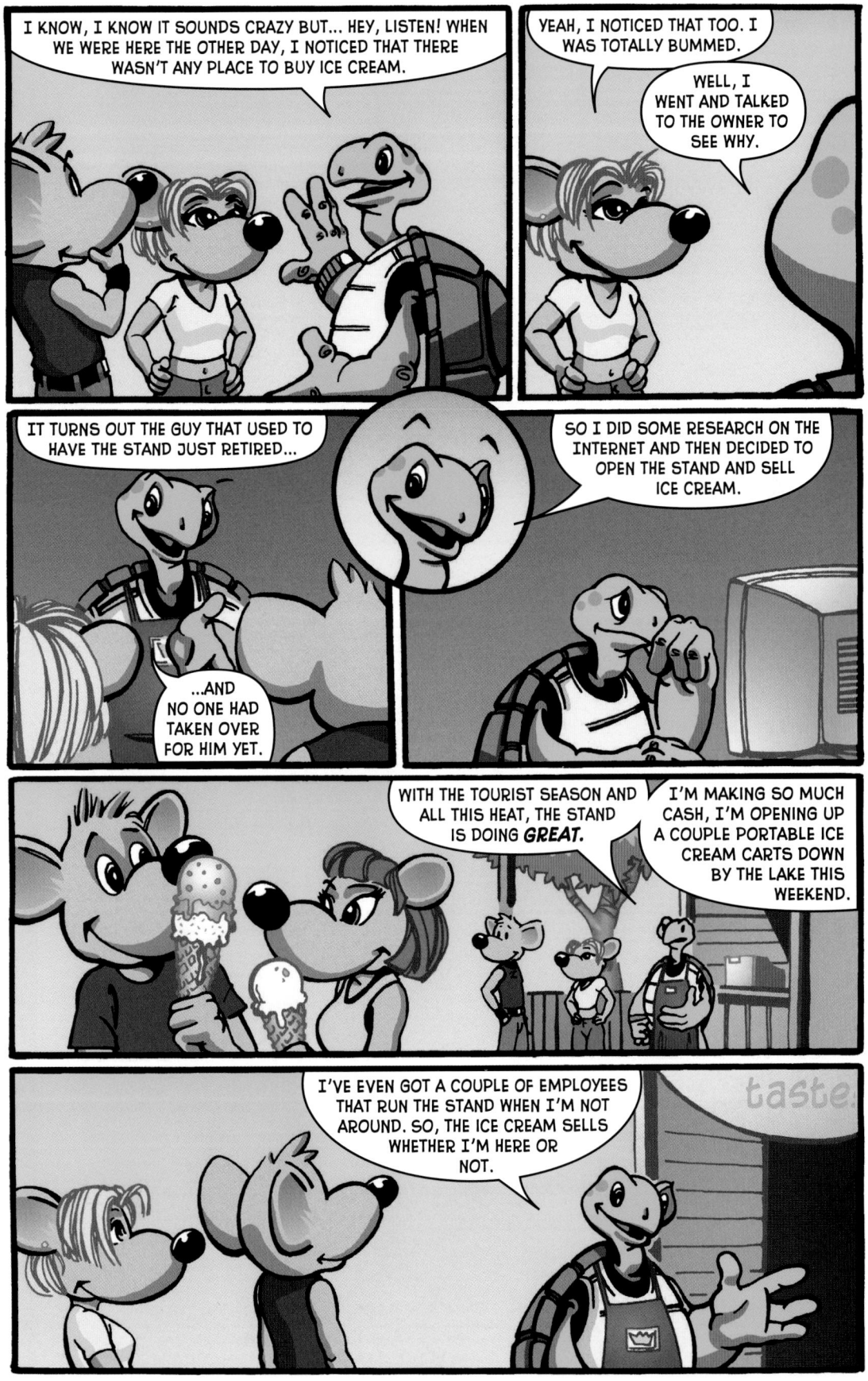
I KNOW, I KNOW IT SOUNDS CRAZY BUT... HEY, LISTEN! WHEN WE WERE HERE THE OTHER DAY, I NOTICED THAT THERE WASN'T ANY PLACE TO BUY ICE CREAM.
YEAH, I NOTICED THAT TOO. I WAS TOTALLY BUMMED.
WELL, I WENT AND TALKED TO THE OWNER TO SEE WHY.
IT TURNS OUT THE GUY THAT USED TO HAVE THE STAND JUST RETIRED...
...AND NO ONE HAD TAKEN OVER FOR HIM YET.
SO I DID SOME RESEARCH ON THE INTERNET AND THEN DECIDED TO OPEN THE STAND AND SELL ICE CREAM.
WITH THE TOURIST SEASON AND ALL THIS HEAT, THE STAND IS DOING GREAT.
I'M MAKING SO MUCH CASH, I'M OPENING UP A COUPLE PORTABLE ICE CREAM CARTS DOWN BY THE LAKE THIS WEEKEND.
I'VE EVEN GOT A COUPLE OF EMPLOYEES THAT RUN THE STAND WHEN I'M NOT AROUND. SO, THE ICE CREAM SELLS WHETHER I'M HERE OR NOT.
taste

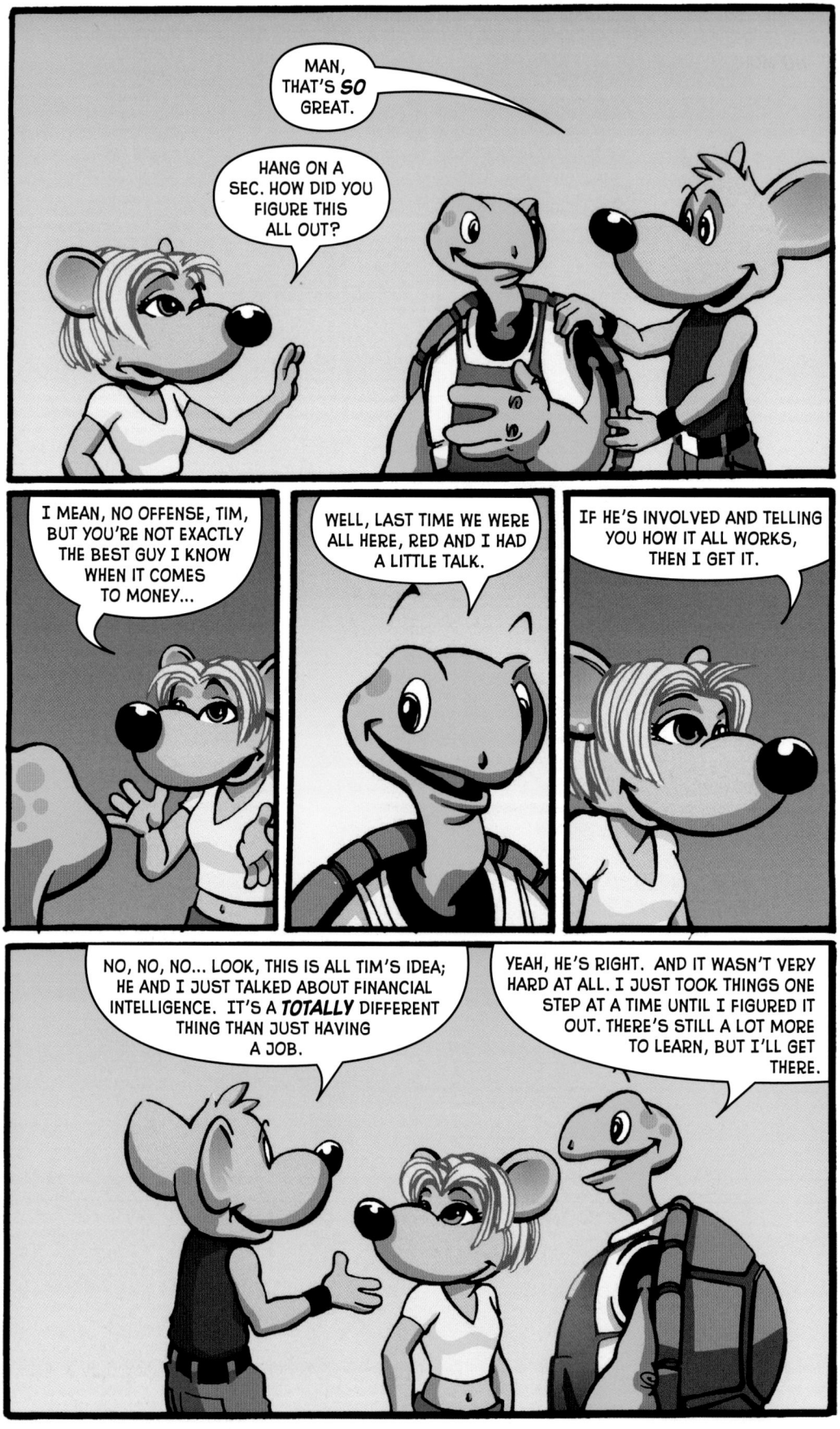
MAN, THAT'S SO GREAT.
HANG ON A SEC. HOW DID YOU FIGURE THIS ALL OUT?
I MEAN, NO OFFENSE, TIM, BUT YOU'RE NOT EXACTLY THE BEST GUY I KNOW WHEN IT COMES TO MONEY...
WELL, LAST TIME WE WERE ALL HERE, RED AND I HAD A LITTLE TALK.
IF HE'S INVOLVED AND TELLING YOU HOW IT ALL WORKS, THEN I GET IT.
NO, NO, NO... LOOK, THIS IS ALL TIM'S IDEA; HE AND I JUST TALKED ABOUT FINANCIAL INTELLIGENCE. IT'S A TOTALLY DIFFERENT THING THAN JUST HAVING A JOB.
YEAH, HE'S RIGHT. AND IT WASN'T VERY HARD AT ALL. I JUST TOOK THINGS ONE STEP AT A TIME UNTIL I FIGURED IT OUT. THERE'S STILL A LOT MORE TO LEARN, BUT I'LL GET THERE.

SO, WAIT A SECOND... YOU WENT FROM HAVING NO MONEY A FEW WEEKS AGO TO HAVING YOUR OWN BUSINESS?
YEAH. MY PARENTS EVEN OFFERED TO HELP ME WITH THE REALLY HARD PARTS. THEY WERE REALLY EXCITED WHEN I TOLD THEM I WAS INTERESTED IN MAKING MONEY AND WHAT MY PLAN WAS.
OK, SO WHAT'S THE STORY, RED? SPILL THE BEANS!
SURE, I'LL BE GLAD TO TELL YOU WHAT I TOLD TIM...
YEAH, IT'S SERIOUSLY COOL STUFF, BUT THERE'S SOMETHING IMPORTANT WE'VE GOTTA TAKE CARE OF FIRST.
OK, LIKE WHAT?
HMM?

WELL, I THINK I HAVE A LONG-OVERDUE DATE WITH THE "ELIMINATOR!"
AND SINCE MY INVESTMENT'S PAYING SO WELL, WE NEED TO CELEBRATE --SO IT'S MY TREAT.
ice crean
UNDER NEW MANAGEMENT
same great taste!
ALL RIGHT!
EXCELLENT! BUT TELL ME ABOUT THIS STUFF AFTER THE RIDE, OK, RED?
IT'S A DEAL!
THE END... AND THE BEGINNING!

About the Author

Robert Kiyosaki

Best known as the author of *Rich Dad Poor Dad*—the #1 personal finance book of all time—Robert Kiyosaki has challenged and changed the way tens of millions of people around the world think about money. He is an entrepreneur, educator, and investor who believes the world needs more entrepreneurs who will create jobs.

With perspectives on money and investing that often contradict conventional wisdom, Robert has earned an international reputation for straight talk, irreverence, and courage and has become a passionate and outspoken advocate for financial education.

Robert and Kim Kiyosaki are founders of The Rich Dad Company, a financial education company, and creators of the *CASHFLOW*® games. In 2013, the company will leverage the global success of the Rich Dad games in the launch of a new and breakthrough offering in mobile and online gaming.

Robert has been heralded as a visionary who has a gift for simplifying complex concepts—ideas related to money, investing, finance, and economics—and has shared his personal journey to financial freedom in ways that resonate with audiences of all ages and backgrounds. His core principles and messages—like "your house is not an asset" and "invest for cash flow" and "savers are losers"—have ignited a firestorm of criticism and ridicule… only to have played out on the world economic stage over the past decade in ways that were both unsettling and prophetic.

His point of view is that "old" advice—go to college, get a good job, save money, get out of debt, invest for the long term, and diversify—has become obsolete advice in today's fast-paced Information Age. His Rich Dad philosophies and messages challenge the status quo. His teachings encourage people to become financially educated and to take an active role in investing for their future.

The author of 19 books, including the international blockbuster *Rich Dad Poor Dad*, Robert has been a featured guest with media outlets in every corner of the world—from CNN, the BBC, Fox News, Al Jazeera, GBTV and PBS, to *Larry King Live, Oprah, Peoples Daily, Sydney Morning Herald, The Doctors, Straits Times, Bloomberg, NPR, USA TODAY,* and hundreds of others—and his books have topped international bestsellers lists for more than a decade. He continues to teach and inspire audiences around the world.

His most recent books include *Unfair Advantage: What Schools Will Never Teach You About Money* and *Midas Touch*, the second book he has co-authored with Donald Trump. Robert's newest book, *Why "A" Students Work for "C" Students,* will be released in April of 2013.

To learn more, visit RichDad.com

Play *CASHFLOW*®

Leading researchers say that we only retain 10% of what we read, but 90% of what we experience. *CASHFLOW* and *CASHFLOW for KIDS* games were created by Robert and Kim Kiyosaki, best-selling authors of *Rich Dad Poor Dad* and *Rich Woman*, to excite others about learning to invest in a fun, experiential way.

Rich Dad *CASHFLOW* games teach you how to achieve financial freedom by working for assets instead of money. You're never too young to learn how to get out of the Rat Race and onto the Fast Track by making money work for you.

Jump-start the financial success of your entire family! Learn the difference between an asset and a liability. Practice real-world investing with play money.

Now you can play the CASHFLOW *game online for FREE!*

Like to play online with others from across the globe? Join the Rich Dad community at richdad.com to play the game for free. No software is required.

Prefer board games? Play the board game at home with your friends and kids. Visit the Rich Dad store at richdad.com

Order your copy at ***richdad.com*** today!

RICH DAD.

Start Your Child Off on the Right Financial Footing

When was the last time your child came home from school talking about what they learned about money? Chances are that your answer is—never.

These two books, ***Rich Dad's Rich Kid Smart Kid*** and ***Rich Dad Poor Dad for Teens,*** introduce parents and teens to the financial world, filling the gap in their education, giving them the right context in which to view money, and placing them on the right financial footing for a secure future.

They will learn:

- How money works
- The difference between assets and liabilities
- To think like an entrepreneur
- How to make wise financial choices
- How to jump-start financial success

Take the first step to ensure your child has a secure financial future with ***Rich Dad's Rich Kid Smart Kid*** and ***Rich Dad Poor Dad for Teens.***

If you are concerned about your child's financial future, you can't afford to pass over these essential books!

Order your copies at ***richdad.com*** today!

RICH DAD.

A *Wall Street Journal* Bestseller, *Rich Dad's CASHFLOW Quadrant*

DON'T LIVE PAYCHECK TO PAYCHECK

In ***Rich Dad's CASHFLOW Quadrant***, the sequel to Robert Kiyosaki's #1 personal-finance book of all time, ***Rich Dad Poor Dad***, you will learn how the role you play in the world of money affects your ability to become financially free. Learn how you can move from being an employee or self-employed to capture the power of being a business owner and investor.

These are the four quadrants of people who make up the world of business

***Rich Dad's CASHFLOW Quadrant* is the perfect guide to getting out of the Rat Race and onto the Fast Track.**

Order your copy at ***richdad.com*** today!

RICH DAD.

Read the Book That Started It All

Rich Dad Poor Dad: What the Rich Teach Their Kids about Money—That the Poor and Middle Class Do Not!

Robert Kiyosaki has challenged and changed the way tens of millions of people around the world think about money. With perspectives that often contradict conventional wisdom, Robert has earned a reputation for straight talk, irreverence, and courage. He is regarded worldwide as a passionate advocate for financial education.

Best
The New York Times
The Wall Street Journal
Business Week
USA TODAY
Seller

***Rich Dad Poor Dad* will...**

- Explode the myth that you need to earn a high income to become rich
- Challenge the belief that your house is an asset
- Show parents why they can't rely on the school system to teach their kids about money
- Define once and for all an asset and a liability
- Teach you what to teach your kids about money for their future financial success

Rich Dad Poor Dad — The #1 Personal Finance Book of All Time!

Order your copy at ***richdad.com*** today!

RICH DAD.

Rich Dad's Wisdom: The Power of Words

To improve your brain's financial power, improve your financial vocabulary. Words are fuel for your brain!

If you improve your financial vocabulary, you will become richer and richer. The good news is that words are free. It does not take money to make money.

Here is an example of the power of words:

Asset - Anything that puts money into your pocket whether or not you work.

Liability - Anything that takes money out of your pocket.

Expand your vocabulary by learning the financial terms in the glossary on the Rich Dad website (**richdad.com**) or get a dictionary of financial terms. As you look up financial words on a regular basis (or look up the definition of a term you hear but do not understand), you may find yourself becoming richer and richer.